CANYONEERING ARIZONA

Hiking and exploring the streambeds,
gorges and slots of Arizona

by Tyler Williams

Funhog Press
Flagstaff, Arizona

The routes described in this book carry a significant risk. In fact, any recreational activity in the outdoors is potentially hazardous. No guidebook, including this one, can alert you to every hazard or replace personal judgement. When you follow any of the routes described in this book, you assume responsibility for your own safety and actions. If you are not prepared to deal with any and all potential hazards found in the outdoors, the author recommends that you do not go into the backcountry.

Change is a constant occurance in nature, and many of the canyons described in this guide have no doubt experienced changes since the descriptions were written. If you should discover any glaring discrepancies between what is described in this guide and what you find, due to natural or man-made causes, please contact the publisher.

Edited by Ginny Gelczis, Bret Simmons
Designed by Mary Williams
Cover photo by Dugald Bremner
Photos by Lisa Gelczis and Tyler Williams

TABLE OF CONTENTS

PREFACE

I have serious reservations about publishing this guidebook. Why should I want to share all these serene and enchanting places with others? Actually, I don't. That is why there are several spectacular canyons out there that you won't find in this book. That is also why, with the exception of just a few, the only canyons in this book are those that have been published previously.

However, encouraging others to visit the wilds has its value. We have already lost some of our most magnificent canyons because they were so wild and unknown that no one knew of their beauty. It is important to give the wilderness a voice by introducing, or at least documenting, our great hinterlands. It is my sincere hope that for every copy of this book sold, we will gain one more advocate for wilderness.

OVERVIEW MAP

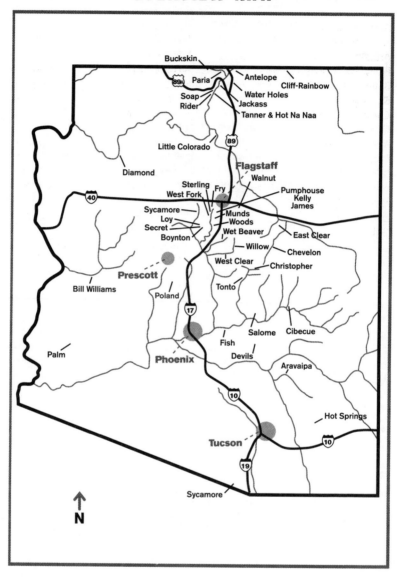

ALPHABETICAL LISTING OF CANYONS

ACKNOWLEDGEMENTS

Writing a guidebook is much more of a group effort than I ever imagined. Numerous people have helped compile the information found in these pages.

Special credit must first be given to my parents. Thanks to my father, who in passing down even a fraction of his determination has provided me with enough of that quality to complete this project. Thanks to my mother, who instilled a love of nature in me at an early age that will stay with me for life. Thanks to Lisa, who took many of the photos for this guide, edited, was my canyoneering partner on many of these routes, and supports my efforts as she has throughout our last eight wonderful years together. This book would definitely not have come to fruition were it not for my cousin Mary Williams. Mary has gone above and beyond her duties as book designer in helping me put it all together. She is truly the producer of this book. Thanks to Ginny Gelczis, who provided a thorough editing job just when I needed it. Jenny Prennace at the USGS library in Flagstaff saved me immeasurable time and energy with her friendly and competent assistance. Ken Webb has good-naturedly dealt with my hair brained schemes over the past 14 years. He also supplied an essential dose of common sense while exploring many of these canyons with me. I am grateful for the advice on authorship and the publishing business given by my friend Mike Shook. Thanks to Jo Deurbrouck, Rose Houck and Glen Rink for help in this area too. Steve Monroe, Kelly Burke, and Andre Potochnik have all steered me in the right direction when I had a geology question. Debra Block kindly answered my queries about map making. During the course of this project, Mitch Diamond expertly guided me out of computer frustration on several occasions, and when the machine finally did die, Chris McIntosh bailed me out by letting me use his computer at a crucial time. Thanks to Kate Thompson for her support and assistance. There are many others that I have failed to mention. Thanks to all of them. I could have never done it alone.

INTRODUCTION

What is Canyoneering?

The word canyoneering has re-emerged in the outdoor lexicon in recent years. The word's first usage, according to Steve Allen in *Canyoneering 3* was by Frederick Dellenbaugh of the 1872 Powell expedition that ran the Colorado River. As river running became more commonplace over the years, the terminology "canyoneering" faded into obscurity. Recently, canyoneering has come back, this time describing the exploration of canyons by foot.

In North America, anyone who walks, hops or swims down a canyon is a canyoneer. This book was written in a manner so as not to scare off recreational hikers by making canyoneering seem too technical. After all, a determined hiker who walks down canyons is a canyoneer.

Europeans have a narrower definition of the sport. In Europe, it is referred to simply as canyoning, and only technical descents qualify as canyoning.

End of the line

There are probably several reasons for the different outlooks on canyoneering between the United States and Europe. One reason might be that Europe does not have the relatively large wilderness areas that North America does. Skills such as route finding and wilderness survival are not a large part of the canyoning equation in Europe, so their focus is on the technical aspects of the sport. Another reason for the broader North American definition is that the word canyoneering has its origins in river running circles, whereas in Europe, canyoning emerged from climbing.

Technical canyoneering techniques are most closely associated with those of spelunking, or caving. Spelunking is essentially canyoneering taken to its logical extreme. Any canyoneer who has squeezed through a slot canyon can relate to the claustrophobia that is so inherent in spelunking. I have heard slot canyons aptly described as "caves without roofs."

Canyoneering does have technical aspects, and these are clearly presented in this book. So where does hiking end and canyoneering begin? There is a lot of gray area here. Does canyoneering start with boulder hopping? with wading or swimming? or is it all simply hiking until a rappel is needed to descend the canyon? As pioneers of the modern era of canyoneering, we are continually defining the sport.

Arizona—The Canyon State

Alaska has its enormous tracts of wilderness, Washington its dense rainforests, and Colorado its high mountain peaks, but no state in this country has more to offer when it comes to canyons than Arizona. From the massive sandstone chasms along the Utah state line to rugged chaparral lined gorges on the Mexican border, Arizona is defined by canyons. No other physical feature of the landscape is as dominant in shaping the geography of the region. To a great extent, canyons in Arizona determine where our roads are laid, our cities are built, and our preserves are established. Canyons carve a dramatic landscape across all of Arizona's geographic provinces.

Arizona's physical geography can be divided into three basic regions: the Colorado Plateau, the Mountains, and the Basin and Range. These regions are used to organize the canyons in this book. The mountain province is dominated by the Mogollon Rim to the northeast, and most of the drainages in this region originate on the rim. Therefore, canyons in this province will be referred to as Mogollon Rim canyons.

The Colorado Plateau is home to possibly the most extensive canyon systems in the world. This region of majestic buttes, colorful cliffs and rocky, sun-baked valleys covers all of northeastern Arizona, as well as much of eastern Utah, western Colorado, and northwestern New Mexico.

A Colorado Plateau scene

Canyons in this region are mostly in sedimentary rock, which is usually sandstone. The canyons of the Colorado Plateau typically have huge, sheer sandstone walls. Walking is very easy along a flat, sandy riverbed, but progress can be impeded by falls and pools. Clear—running streams are a rarity, but they do occur. Usually the only water encountered in these canyons is an occasional unappealing brown scum-filled pool. However, the narrows of the Colorado Plateau canyons are some of the best in the world. Convoluted, extremely narrow passageways are common. Flash flood danger is generally more severe in these canyons than in canyons of other regions.

The Mogollon Rim is a dramatic escarpment running generally from the northwest to the southeast across the middle of Arizona. It is the southern edge of the mighty Colorado Plateau. Referred to as simply "the rim" by Arizonans, it rises from the juniper covered flats near Ash Fork and appears as an eastward running rise near Bill Williams Mountain in northern Arizona. By the time it reaches the Sedona area, the rim is an obvious cliff of white, brown, and red rock dropping straight to the valley floor. Just east of Sedona, the rim makes an abrupt turn to the south, and morphs into a gently sloping grade, as old lava flows cover the underlying geology.

Mountainous terrain below the Mogollon Rim

In the vicinity of Strawberry, Arizona, it once again turns nearly due east and becomes a prominent rim. By the time it reaches Pinetop, it is again guised in its appearance as it blends with the rise of the White Mountains. At the southern edge of the White Mountains, near the town of Hannagan Meadow, the Mogollon Rim pokes out of the rolling hillsides of spruce and makes a final grand presentation before dropping off into the hill country of the Blue River.

The canyons of the Mogollon Rim are as varied as the environments they connect. From the lush forests of the rim to the warm and sunny Sonoran Desert, canyons of the Mogollon Rim have it all. Vegetation is a big attraction in these canyons. The shade of canyon rims provides a cool environment where a multitude of plants flourish. Many Mogollon Rim canyons are blessed with perennial water, making waterfalls and clear deep pools inviting places on hot days. This fruitful environment provides ideal habitats for wildlife. The only three bears I have ever seen in Arizona have all been lurking in Mogollon Rim canyons.

The geology of the western Mogollon Rim is fairly consistent and simple. Basalt covers the rims, sometimes forming defiant bands of rimrock, but usually not posing any problems in the canyon bottoms. Coconino sandstone is the buff to white colored sandstone usually directly below the basalt. This layer often creates the most difficulty, and the most beauty. Large falls, as well as a few pools, may be found in the Coconino. Below the Coconino is the Supai sandstone, the red rock that has made Sedona so famous. In the Supai, big falls are rare, but stunningly beautiful pools and quaint little narrows can be found.

The geology of the central and eastern portions of the rim is much more complex, with igneous and metamorphic rock bands intruding an otherwise simple geologic groundwork.

The Basin and Range province dominates much of the western United States. It extends from southern Oregon in the north to northern Mexico in the south, and from the Sierras of California in the west to the Wasatch

Basin and range topography

Front of Utah in the east. Basin and range covers most of the western and southern portions of Arizona. Arizona basin and range country is a series of mountain ranges running generally south to north. Between these ranges are broad valleys, or basins. In southeastern Arizona, the basins are sweeping grasslands. In southwestern Arizona, they are some of the hottest and driest deserts on earth.

Canyons in this region are generally oases in the desert. Dense riparian vegetation and cool streams fill the canyon bottoms, usually below canyon walls covered in saguaro and cholla cactus. The technical difficulty of these canyons is less than that of Mogollon Rim or Colorado Plateau canyons. All three rock types—igneous, sedimentary, and metamorphic—are found in the canyons of the Basin and Range.

Canyoneering Techniques

"On each side rose the canyon walls, roughly perpendicular. There was no way to continue except by dropping into the pool. I hesitated. Beyond this point there could hardly be any returning, yet the main canyon was still not visible below. Obviously the only sensible thing to do was to turn back. I edged over the lip of stone and dropped feet first into the water." - Edward Abbey

Canyoneering is a term that has surfaced in recent years for the hybrid of skills used in descending canyons. There are three core skills needed in canyoneering, they are: climbing, swimming, and route finding.

Climbing is one of the oldest outdoor pursuits and it has an elaborate rating system. Basically, climbing is broken into five grades of difficulty. The fifth class is additionally broken down using decimal points; 5.1, 5.2 and so on. In this day and age, the first four classes of difficulty are hardly even referred to as climbing anymore. What is referred to as scrambling in this book is equivalent to grade 3 or 4 climbing. Fifth class climbing begins when a fall would cause serious injury or death. Of course,

Climbing

the seriousness of any fall is closely related to its height. Class 4 scrambles with great exposure could also be fatal. Climbing a vertical extension ladder to the second story would be the equivalent of an easy (5.0, 5.1) fifth class climb. The upper limits of the sport are now rated 5.15. This is truly spider-man stuff, overhanging walls with fingerholds only millimeters wide. The hardest climbing moves in this book are a 5.6 or so. Most of the climbing necessary to descend the canyons in this book is grade 4, or scrambling. If a route in this book requires a climb of fifth class difficulty, this will be mentioned in the trip description.

Scrambling can probably best be thought of as very steep hiking. Hiking ends and scrambling begins when one must use his hands, not just his feet, to get through the terrain. Many of us will want a safety rope for scrambles with exposure.

Lisa Gelczis

Boulder hopping

Boulder hopping is another discipline of canyoneering. Boulder hopping is fairly self explanatory—it means hopping from boulder to boulder. Boulder hopping takes balance, agility, and a certain amount of ankle strength. It gets particularly interesting when the boulders are loose or slick with moisture. As a progression of difficulty, hiking becomes boulder hopping, boulder hopping advances to scrambling, and scrambling evolves into climbing.

Since canyon bottoms are where **water** tends to end up, dealing with this medium is a big part of canyoneering. Of course, the water in the canyon is often the attraction of the place.

Wading is common in all but the driest of canyons, and it should not be looked on with disdain. Embrace the water and get those shoes wet! Trying to scale the canyon walls in order to avoid wet feet will usually cause more trouble than it will save. As wades get above waist level things get more complicated. If you have a pack, carry it over your head. Don't wait until you drop off that ledge into shoulder deep water to find that your pack isn't waterproof. If you're wearing a cotton shirt, take it off before entering the pool. You'll probably want it nice and dry on the other side.

Mike Kuhns

Drysuits are excellent for swimming cold pools, but you
must be careful not to puncture them.

Swimming can be surprisingly difficult when the water is cold. In Arizona's
canyons, the water temperature is often less than 60 degrees. Even a
strong and athletic person can be numbed to the point of drowning if the
water is cold enough and the swim is long enough. Of course, it is always
best to attempt well-watered canyons when the air temperature is <u>hot</u>.

Drysuits and wetsuits can help a great deal when swimming cold pools.
Drysuits are best—with rubber gaskets at the neck, wrists, and ankles and
waterproof material throughout, your body stays completely dry. A drysuit
can greatly reduce your risk of hypothermia and make swimming across a
cold pool much more enjoyable. Wetsuits are good too. Though not as
warm as a drysuit, a wetsuit insulates and holds up better to abrasion
when you're hiking between pools.

The question of how to best manage your pack when swimming has seen a
multitude of approaches over the years. I started out using an inflated air
mattress tied to my pack. When faced with a pool crossing, I would lay the
air mattress on the water with my pack on top and proceed to push the
floating barge in front of me as I swam. This is not an entirely bad technique, though the mattress inevitably springs a leak and the pack tends to
slide off into the water. A much preferred technique is to use a drybag. I
know what you're thinking—more gear, more money, but a $25 drybag is
cheaper than the dozen air mattresses you'll go through in as many trips.
A rubber drybag will fit most of your supplies; certainly the essentials that
need to stay dry. Pack your gear into the drybag, put the drybag into your
pack, and that is it, nothing to inflate, nothing to puncture, and no more
cumbersome than what you would normally backpack with. Most back-
packs will float well with a large drybag in them, the only exception possibly being certain big external frame packs. When faced with a long pool,

you can throw your pack far out in front of you and swim unencumbered. New all rubber drybag/backpack canyoneering packs are now starting to make their way to the market. I highly recommend them, as they keep all your gear dry and float even better than a drybag-filled backpack.

Anyone who has walked from point A to point B without signs or a trail leading the way has done some route finding. **Route finding** is picking a path of travel that will lead to your destination. In canyoneering, route finding is used in several ways: finding the canyon itself, without a trail leading you to it; finding a slope which allows access either in of out of a canyon; and finding routes around pools or falls that may obstruct the main canyon bottom.

Making your way to a canyon rim, or back to your car from a canyon rim, requires a good sense of direction more than anything else. A good map and a compass are essentials.

Getting around pools or falls is another aspect of route finding where faults and slopes of colluvium are good things to look for. Remember, though, that descending the canyon bottom is by definition canyoneering, so try to be prepared to descend the falls, swim the pools, and squeeze through the narrows before setting out on a canyoneering trip.

Route finding

Finding a route into or out of a canyon can be a slow trial and error process. I have tried to explain where the necessary routes are for the canyons in this book, hopefully eliminating the trial and error aspect of route finding for you. However, here are a few general hints regarding routes.

• Faults often create a break in cliffbands, forming a steep gully which may serve as a route amidst otherwise vertical rock. Look at the stratigraphy (the layers) of a canyon wall, and try to find a spot where it is displaced. This is a fault, and there may be a route here.

• Colluvium is the collection of rocks which accumulate at the base of cliffs. Huge slopes of colluvium are often good places for routes. When trying to find routes in canyon country, binoculars are a handy tool. The deceptive scale, especially of the Colorado Plateau canyons, can make a wide ledge look like a climber's fingerhold at a distance, and a closer view is helpful.

• A keen eye for cairns is also a good skill, as most routes are marked with these stacks of rocks.

Rappelling is the most technical of canyoneering skills. I won't go into great detail about how to rappel here. If you don't have experience rappelling, seek qualified instruction and practice, practice, practice before setting out. Your life depends on your knowledge and skill. I highly recommend going with a guide on technical descents. Believe me, it's no fun to be two hours into a canyon, standing atop a 50 foot cliff and asking, "how does this rope go through here again?"

Here are a few tips on canyoneering rappels:

• When rappelling with a heavy pack, don't rappel with it on your back. Either lower it down to your partner or rappel with it clipped to your harness between your legs. It's more stable and out of the way to have the weight below you than on your back pulling you backwards.

• Scout out your landing area well before you get there. Sometimes falls terminate in potholes or deep pools, and a short pendulum can get you to a much better landing spot.

Rappelling

• It may seem obvious, but always bring enough rope! Remember, only those who have made their way into a sheer-walled gorge with no way out but downstream know the meaning of commitment.

Do Your Part

"Half the world hates what half the world does every day."
-Neil Peart of RUSH

If you can take the time to enjoy the canyon country of Arizona, you should be able to take some time to preserve it as well. I can't get on too high of a stump here, because I know I don't do all I could to save our wild areas. But there are some basic things we can and should do to defend the wilderness we explore.

Whether it is a dam being built, a road being paved, or a tree being felled, someone is responsible for the carnage. It is our job to find out who, and to oppose them at every opportunity. Be aware of your representative's voting record on environmental issues. Get involved with local environmental organizations. If it comes to it, create your own grassroots organization for a specific cause. As Margaret Mead said, "Never doubt that a small group of thoughtful, committed citizens can change the world. Indeed, it is the only thing that ever has."

Before we divide the world into right vs. wrong, though, we must remind ourselves of this: As consumers and users of computers, televisions, washing machines, refrigerators, air conditioners, cars, airplanes, motorboats, motorcycles, chairlifts, casinos, lawn mowers and leaf blowers, we are all guilty for the fouling of our environment.

And so, maybe it is the natural course of things to despoil our planet and in turn exterminate ourselves. Extinction will happen soon enough to us humans, as it does with all species. We are just a blip on the screen of geologic time, and the canyons will live on long after every human has died and been swallowed by the soil. The human race is just a mild infection, noticed only for a few days in the life of planet Earth.

Given this perspective, it might be easy to think that our actions mean very little. A beer can tossed thoughtlessly on the side of the road, or even a dam drowning a beautiful canyon, won't be noticed in a million years. This rationale is both lazy and apathetic, despite being factually true.

So as a gesture of consideration for others (fellow canyoneers, animals, grandchildren), and as a selfish action designed to preserve things as we know and enjoy them, we all ought to make some effort to preserve our natural world, including our canyons. For the big picture, join one of the many environmental groups out there. On a smaller scale, clean up after yourself, and others, when exploring canyons.

Backcountry Ethics

"Leave only footprints, take only photographs and memories." I wish I could end this chapter right there. However, as pervasive as this and other sayings such as "pack it in, pack it out" seem to be, the habits of some backcountry users continue to be almost antithetical to these dictums. Beer cans piled high in fire rings, toilet paper strewn about the forest, and limbs cut off live trees are constant reminders that people are in need of backcountry education. I wrote this book with great trepidation, fearing that it might lead to overuse of our wild canyons. Though this guide may bring more people into Arizona's canyons, my hope is that those people will be stewards, rather than exploiters, of the land. "More people" is generally a negative term to wilderness lovers, but if it means more people cleaning up trashed campsites, more people fighting to save our canyons, and more people promoting good backcountry ethics, it can be a positive term. The "more people" I'm referring to is you, the guidebook user. I plead for you to take care of these places.

If you see people acting ignorantly—shooting a cactus or tree, breaking a bottle, or littering, it is your job to educate them about their behavior. If education is a daunting task (for example, if the offender is really big, really drunk, and really well armed), you can always try to get a license plate number and report it to the forest service or other managing agency. They will follow up on your report, and a stiff fine could be levied, which might make the ignorant one think about his actions next time.

In the good ol' days, "leave no trace" camping techniques weren't as important as they are today. There was a time when only one person a year would visit your favorite backcountry camp. Those days are gone. Now one person a week visits that same camp. Simply our presence in the backcountry is an intrusion, so we must take steps to make that intrusion as little as possible.

As our population continues to soar into the 21st century, we must impose rules on ourselves. Those rules applied to the backcountry are known as "leave no trace" techniques. The best rule of thumb regarding "leave no trace" is this: Treat the land as if it were your home. After all, when you are out there, it is your home. Be diligent to always leave a site at least as clean and natural looking as when you found it.

Campfires The first thing most wilderness travellers (including me) do when they make camp is establish a fire spot, and commence to build one. The most popular backcountry axiom these days is that campfires are bad. Though there are several good reasons not to have a campfire—smoke in the eyes, sparks burning holes in your new $400 North Face parka, firelight muting the beautiful night sky, I'm not going to tell you not to have one. If you elect not to have a campfire, good on you, "you're a better man than I, Gunga Din." If you do have one, at least be sensitive about it.

Fire rings are okay to use if they already exist, but for heaven's sake don't make any new ones. There are more than enough out there already. Fire rings tend to attract trash, and campsites are generally nicer without one. Stoves are nicer to cook on. Remember, campfires are not synonymous with camping.

If you're camping at a site with no ring, and you must have a fire, dig a hole or clear a bare spot for your fire. When the fire has burned down to ashes, put it out thoroughly with water and either bury the ashes or scatter them away from camp. Also, scatter any big chunks of charcoal, though there shouldn't be any left if you let the fire burn down completely.

Don't build a fire next to a cliff wall. Though it is a romantic scene—the bearded mountain man, dressed in buckskins and cradling his rifle, sitting with his back to the canyon wall while the fire burns warmly next to him, heating the sandstone against his back—smoke from fires makes ugly black stains on canyon walls. I've even seen magnificent pictograph panels obscured by the soot from a cliffside campfire.

When you're gathering fuel for the fire, there's no need to unleash your fury on the surrounding green forest by chopping live trees. Burn only dead and down wood. Stay away from the "all-nighter" log, it will be a smoldering, half-burned, blackened mess in the morning. In many of Arizona's canyons, driftwood left behind from floods makes an excellent source of firewood.

Finally, glass, metal, foil, and anything else that won't turn to ash does not belong! Don't put these things in your fire thinking they will disappear. You must pack them out!

Trash Litter, garbage, rubbish, trash, whatever you call it, it is something that does not belong in the great outdoors. I can hardly think of anything more disrespectful than leaving behind personal trash where someone else will have to clean it up after you. I don't suppose I'll ever understand the mentality behind litterbugs—a much too glossy term for the bufoons. I guess it is simply laziness that compels people (I'm being generous with the term "people") to leave their messes for the rest of us. Whatever slobbish behavior is conducted at home is their business, but we should all take personal offense when that slobbish behavior is thrust into our palaces of nature. It doesn't end there; even trash from communities can make it into our canyons. Anything littered near a streambed gets washed downstream during high water, only to get lodged in a strainer deep in a wilderness canyon's narrows.

If you see litter in our backcountry, pick it up. If you get the rare opportunity to actually see a litterbug in action, make sure they are enlightened to their stupidity. On the issue of trash, "If you are not part of the solution, you are part of the problem."

Crap When nature calls in the backcountry, once again, treat the wilderness as if it were your home. You wouldn't defecate near your water supply, or in your front yard. Follow some logical guidelines: Always go at least 100 yards from water. Dig a hole about six inches deep (a stick, rock, or boot is usually a sufficient tool for digging), and bury your feces. Don't bury toilet paper. Burn it completely or pack it out.

Arizona's Climate

If you were to ask the average American to describe Arizona's climate in one word, their answer would probably be *hot*. For those of us who live in the Grand Canyon state, however, we know that the correct answer would be *varied*. From scorching deserts to frigid mountains, Arizona has several climatic zones and accordingly, quite variable weather. Anyone driving the 2.5 hours from Phoenix to Flagstaff can see and feel the vast weather changes that are common to our state. I'll never forget the time I drove through Phoenix in oppressive 100 degree heat with no air conditioning. With the windows rolled down at 70 m.p.h., I still had to continually pour cold water on myself to stay comfortable. Only two hours later, the windows were all rolled up and the car's heat was on as I drove into Flagstaff. There was white stuff on the ground (hail, not snow), and the temperature was a damp 49 degrees.

The main reason for this wide range of climates in our state is elevation. As you go up in elevation, the temperature decreases by about 3.5 degrees every 1000 feet. This effect, called the *lapse rate*, combined with other local weather effects, produces the vast differences in Arizona weather.

Topography also affects Arizona's weather. The northeastern deserts of the Colorado Plateau are much drier than locations to the south at corresponding elevations. Notice on the following climate charts, the differences between Leupp and Sedona. Both of these locations are at approximately the same elevation, and only about 50 air miles apart, yet Sedona has a decidedly wetter, more moderate climate. This illustrates how the Mogollon Rim, San Francisco Peaks, and Kaibab Plateau block moisture from reaching the arid northeastern deserts.

Some of the greatest precipitation falls over the central mountain ranges of the state. As storms move across our region from the south or west, these ranges are the first barriers the storms hit, causing copious amounts of rain or snow to fall. Crown King, in the southern Bradshaw Mountains, receives

Climate Charts

To give you an idea of what weather to expect in a certain canyon in a given month, here are some monthly averages for selected locations around the state. The initials "tr" stand for trace. Everything else is self-explanatory.

Flagstaff elevation 7006'

	Jan	Feb	Mar	Apr	May	Jun	Jul	Aug	Sep	Oct	Nov	Dec	Total
high	41	44	49	57	66	78	81	79	73	63	51	42	
low	15	17	20	25	32	40	50	49	41	30	21	16	
snow	20	18	23	10	2	tr	tr	tr	tr	2	10	16	100"
precip	2.1	2.0	2.1	1.4	0.8	0.6	2.5	2.6	1.5	1.5	1.7	2.3	21.0"

Sedona elevation 4500'

	Jan	Feb	Mar	Apr	May	Jun	Jul	Aug	Sep	Oct	Nov	Dec	Total
high	55	60	64	73	81	92	96	93	89	78	65	56	
low	29	32	35	41	47	56	64	62	57	47	36	30	
snow	2	1	1	tr	0	0	0	0	0	0	tr	2	6"
precip	2.0	1.7	1.9	1.1	0.6	0.5	1.9	2.1	1.5	1.5	1.4	1.5	17.7"

Canyon De Chelly elevation 5500'

	Jan	Feb	Mar	Apr	May	Jun	Jul	Aug	Sep	Oct	Nov	Dec	Total
high	44	51	58	68	78	88	89	89	84	71	56	46	
low	18	22	26	34	43	51	60	58	49	36	25	18	
snow	3	3	2	1	tr	0	0	0	0	tr	1	4	14"
precip	0.6	0.4	0.7	0.6	0.5	0.3	1.3	1.7	0.9	1.1	0.6	0.6	9.3"

Payson elevation 5000'

	Jan	Feb	Mar	Apr	May	Jun	Jul	Aug	Sep	Oct	Nov	Dec	Total
high	53	55	61	69	78	87	90	87	83	74	62	54	
low	19	22	26	31	36	44	56	55	47	36	25	20	
snow	6	5	3	1	tr	0	0	0	0	tr	1	5	21"
precip	1.9	2.0	1.9	1.0	0.4	0.5	2.5	3.1	2.0	1.6	1.5	2.1	20.6"

Leupp elevation 4700'

	Jan	Feb	Mar	Apr	May	Jun	Jul	Aug	Sep	Oct	Nov	Dec	Total
high	47	55	62	72	81	91	95	92	87	75	60	48	
low	16	20	25	34	41	49	59	57	48	36	24	17	
snow	2	1	1	0	0	0	0	0	0	tr	tr	3	6"
precip	0.4	0.3	0.4	0.3	0.2	0.4	1.1	1.1	0.8	0.7	0.3	0.4	6.3"

Fort Huachuca elevation 4664'

	Jan	Feb	Mar	Apr	May	Jun	Jul	Aug	Sep	Oct	Nov	Dec	Total
high	58	61	66	74	82	90	89	86	84	77	67	60	
low	34	36	40	47	55	64	66	65	61	52	41	36	
snow	1	2	2	tr	0	0	0	0	0	tr	1	1	7"
precip	0.7	0.6	0.5	0.2	0.1	0.4	4.5	3.9	1.6	0.7	0.4	1.0	14.6"

Tucson elevation 2584'

	Jan	Feb	Mar	Apr	May	Jun	Jul	Aug	Sep	Oct	Nov	Dec	Total
high	63	68	72	81	89	99	99	96	94	83	72	64	
low	39	40	44	51	58	69	73	71	67	58	45	39	
snow	tr	tr	tr	tr	0	0	0	0	0	0	tr	tr	2"
precip	0.9	0.7	0.7	0.3	0.1	0.2	2.5	2.2	1.4	0.9	0.6	0.9	11.8"

Phoenix elevation 1110'

	Jan	Feb	Mar	Apr	May	Jun	Jul	Aug	Sep	Oct	Nov	Dec	Total
high	64	70	74	82	91	101	104	101	99	89	73	65	
low	40	41	47	51	61	70	79	78	70	59	48	40	
snow	tr	tr	0	0	0	0	0	0	0	0	0	tr	tr"
precip	0.7	0.6	0.8	0.3	0.1	0.1	0.8	1.0	0.7	0.6	0.6	0.9	7.3"

the most precipitation in the state, on average, with 28 inches a year. The most precipitation ever to fall in 24 hours in Arizona is 11.4 inches of rain. This occurred at Workman Creek in the Sierra Anchas on September 4, 1970.

Arizona rarely has a "normal" year weatherwise. It is either flood or drought, heat wave or cold snap. With that said, here is a general synopsis of Arizona's seasons and how they affect canyoneering.

Arizona basically has two wet seasons—winter and summer—and two dry seasons—spring and fall. Winter precipitation results from low pressure systems moving into the state from the west. These storms usually produce steady drizzles in the southern deserts, snow in the central and northern mountains, and scattered snow and wind in the northern deserts. Winter storms generally begin to roll into the state in November and continue to come through at varying intervals until early April.

November is a nice time of year in many Arizona canyons. Fall colors are ablaze through November, and desert temperatures are warm and pleasant. Canyons at high elevations usually get snowed in by the end of the month. **December** and **January** are the heart of winter. Periods of high pressure between storm systems can provide beautiful crisp and clear hiking weather for desert canyons. Sunlight never penetrates narrow canyons in mid-winter, so places like Buckskin Gulch are iceboxes. **February** shows the first signs of spring in the Sonoran Desert. The wildflowers begin to bloom. Beware of floods. Canyons that drain the high country flood from rain on the snowpack or sudden warm weather most often in February and March. **March** is the start of spring in Arizona, and probably our most volatile month. A week of sunny warm weather can be followed by a big winter storm. Phoenix has been as cold as 25 degrees and as hot as 100 degrees in this month. The driest time of the year in Arizona is the spring. The southern part of the state has a more pronounced and earlier arriving spring dry season than the north. **April** is usually pleasant in the south, whereas storm systems can still move through northern Arizona into **May**. Springtime often finds incessant winds in the northern deserts. **June** is a hot and dry month. This is the time to explore narrow, wet canyons. The temperatures are hot, but the thunderstorms of summer haven't started yet, so flash flood danger is minimal. **July** ushers in the monsoon season. Usually starting around mid-month, subtropical moisture moves into the state from the south, creating thunderstorms. Because the moisture comes from the south, southern Arizona receives a stronger monsoon than the north, but the entire state is affected. Nearly every location in Arizona receives its maximum monthly precipitation in July or August. **August** is the heart of monsoon season. Flash flood danger is ever-present. **September** has lingering rains in the first half of the month, with gorgeous warm fall weather typical towards the end of the month. September can be quite rainy or quite dry. It is a transition month. This is your last chance to explore most wet canyons without a wetsuit or drysuit, because temperatures are quickly descending into autumn. **October** is the hiking month. Fall colors are beginning to peek through in many canyon bottoms. Temperatures are mild across the state, from upper 80s in the hottest deserts to the upper 50s in the mountains. Though it is generally thought of as a dry month, radical weather can occur. Flagstaff's second wettest month ever recorded was October of 1972, when it received 9.9 inches of precipitation.

Early Arizonans

Arizona's first human inhabitants were known as the Archaics. They roamed the colder, wetter, post ice-age landscape around 6000 B.C. These original Arizona natives fit the classic "cave-man" image. Dressed in skins and toting spears, the Archaics hunted mammoths and giant sloths. By 2000 B.C. the climate had changed, and so had the Archaics. Though hunting was still their forté, they began to rely on gathering nuts and a few scant fruits to supplement their diet. Over the next 50 generations or so, the Archaics gradually turned to more of a soil-based society. By 500 B.C., they were farming more extensively, mainly due to the emergence of a new vegetable that had arrived from the south—corn.

These ancient hunter-gatherers were the forbearers to five main cultures that continued to thrive in Arizona until the 1400s—the Anasazi, Mogollon, Sinagua, Hohokam, and Salado.

You might stumble across ruins left from the **Anasazi** while exploring canyons on the Colorado Plateau. This culture is responsible for building the dramatic cliff dwellings that pepper their ancestral home of the four corners region. Places like Mesa Verde National Park, Navajo National Monument, Keet Seel, and Canyon De Chelly all showcase relics of the Anasazi people. The Anasazi did not build these elaborate apartments right away, though.

In the early stages of their culture, around 100 A.D., pithouses were the shelter of choice. A typical pithouse was square, or circular, and dug a few feet into the ground. Rocks imbedded in the walls provided stability. Beefy tree limbs served as support beams for the roof, which was a crosshatch of smaller limbs, brush, grass, bark, and mud. Pithouses were used by all the cultures in ancient Arizona. The pithouse was the 3-bedroom, 2-bath of its day.

One can only live in a dark, damp, subterranean hovel for so long, though. Around 700 A.D., the Anasazi began building the elaborate cliff dwellings like the ones preserved at Canyon De Chelly. The culture thrived for another 600 years. The Anasazi made pottery, irrigated farms, and built entire cities, like the one found at Chaco Canyon in New Mexico.

Then, about the year 1300, the Anasazi left. Reasons for their departure are a constant subject for speculation. Drought was probably part of it. Family by family, the Anasazi evacuated the arid four corners region for new homes to the east and south, settling in pueblos along the Rio Grande, Puerco, and Little Colorado Rivers. The Hopis are descendants of this great culture, still living in the majestic sandstone country of the Colorado Plateau.

The Hopis are descendants of another great culture as well—the **Sinagua**. The Sinaguans lived near the Flagstaff area and south into the Verde Valley. The first traces of this culture date back to about 600 A.D. During this time, the Sinaguans were segmented into two groups: the Northerns, who lived near present-day Flagstaff, and the Southerns, who dwelled closer to present-day Sedona.

Between 1100 and 1200 A.D., the Sinaguan culture boomed. They moved from pithouses to elaborate pueblos, traded extensively with other societies like the Anasazi and Hohokam, and built structures for ceremony and sport. One theory contends that this cultural boom was brought on by the eruption of Sunset Crater near Flagstaff in 1064. The ash deposited from the volcano created fertile ground in Sinaguan land, which in turn created a "land rush" immigration to the area from tribes throughout the Southwest. The fruitful farming and mix of cultures promoted cultural prosperity.

Following this "classic" Sinaguan period, the Northern Sinaguans moved south, to join their neighbors in the accommodating Verde Valley near

Lisa Gelczis

Petroglyphs

today's Sedona. Life here must have been good around 1300, with ample water and a moderate climate providing ideal conditions for Sinaguan life.

By 1400, the Sinaguans began to drift out of the Verde Valley. It is difficult to interpret what precipitates an exodus by an entire culture, but disease is a common speculation, and it might have been a primary factor here. By 1425, the Sinaguans were all gone. Left behind were the ruins of Tuzigoot and Montezuma Castle, as well as Walnut Canyon and Wupatki. You are likely to spot ancient ruins of the Sinaguans in many of the Mogollon Rim canyons which lie to the north of West Clear Creek.

Moving southeastward along the Mogollon Rim from West Clear Creek, you might discover onetime dwellings of the **Mogollon** people. The Mogollons lived along the rim of the same name in round pithouses until about 900 A.D., when they changed their living quarters to Anasazi-influenced above ground pueblos. This architectural shift is one of the few changes the Mogollons made in their 1500-year tenure along the rim. This civilization kept it simple. They did not abandon their hunting and gathering roots for elaborately irrigated farming. Rather, the Mogollon subsisted mostly on the meat of deer, squirrel, antelope and rabbit. The Mogollons roamed the drainages of the Salt and Gila rivers until 1400. Climate estimates indicate that a drought in the mid-1300s might have led to their leaving the rim country. There is some speculation that the Mogollon are the ancestors of the Tarahumara Indians in northern Mexico.

Two thousand years ago, the people living in northern Mexico were the **Hohokam**. These desert dwelling people ranged across the Sonoran Desert, but primarily lived in the Salt and Gila river valleys, the site of today's Phoenix. The Hohokam were impressive canal builders, flooding their fields of corn, barley, squash, beans, and even cotton with the fresh mountain snowmelt that would come coursing into the desert each spring. However, if the rivers brought them life, they were also their bane. Streambed sediment records indicate that during the Hohokam's cultural peak around 1360, a 450-year flood came roaring down the Salt River, wiping out their elaborate irrigation systems and forcing them to relocate.

The culture ended around 1450, splintering into groups that would form the Pima and Tohono O'odham tribes of today. Much of the Hohokam's history has been lost or paved over with the growth of the Phoenix area.

Also lost to modern man are the ruins of the **Salado**. Most of them are under Roosevelt Lake, which covers the once fertile lower Tonto Basin. This culture was the melting pot of early Arizona inhabitants. Traits of the Anasazi, Mogollon, and Hohokam people all mingled here, leading some archaeologists to believe that the Salado was not its own culture, but just an overlapping area of several different cultures. In any case, the mix of cultures might have helped create a varied, healthy diet for the people of the Tonto Basin. Skeletons at Salado sites show no signs of nutritional distress, as is common among other southwestern tribes. Think of the Salado people when descending canyons like Tonto and Salome creeks. These wild, beautiful places were once the Salado's backyard.

Traces of Arizona's ancient cultures are seen in many environments, but especially in our canyons. Before we had the power and audacity to build giant aqueducts across deserts, people tended to live near water. Since water collects in canyon bottoms, this is a good place to find ruins.
Ruins are an integral part of Arizona's canyons. As guardians of our canyons, canyoneers must also be caretakers of our links with the past. Visiting ruins in the wilderness is a privilege granted to those of us that make the effort to get there. Don't treat them with the respect a roadside tourist attraction would receive. Treat a ruin like a museum, because that is essentially what it is. Don't climb on walls of ruins, don't camp in them, and certainly don't build fires in or near ruins or petroglyph panels. I have seen more than one panel of petroglyphs obliterated by soot from a fire. Artifacts such as baskets, pottery and pottery shards should be left where they are. It is a federal offense to remove any of these things, or to damage an archaeological site in any way.

HOW TO USE THIS BOOK

Canyons are arranged throughout this book geographically from northwest to southeast. Refer to the state map or table of contents to find a particular canyon.

PLEASE READ THIS
No, your other left!

Directions in this book are always given as if you were looking downstream. If a feature is said to be on the right, this means it is on the right side of the creekbed **if you were looking downstream, regardless of which way you might actually be looking or travelling.** So, if you are hiking upstream, and you are searching for something said to be on the right, where will it be? On your right or your left? If you said left, you were right, oops, I mean, correct.

Perhaps you've run into this convention before. Ever heard of skier's left or right? It means as a skier is looking downhill. River runners always use this left and right rule too, it prevents confusion. In canyoneering, like river running and skiing, things are referred to as you would see them looking downstream or downhill. Sometimes directions will be stated as creek right, or river left, this is just a way of reminding ourselves of the rule of rights and lefts.

Best Season

This is what I consider to be the nicest time of year for a particular trip. However, the months I have listed are just a guideline. The weather varies tremendously from year to year in Arizona, so be aware of what the weather has been doing, and plan accordingly. Of course, dedicated canyoneers can extend the season of any trip. For instance, the use of drysuits can extend the season for wet canyons. Flash flood danger is often a consideration, which is why many canyons are to be avoided during the thunderstorm season from July through September.

Elevation

Listed are the highest and lowest elevations, in feet, found on the described route. If there is much swimming or wading in the canyon, and creek elevations are significantly lower than those found at the start of the route, creek elevations will be listed separately. Many elevations are rounded to the nearest 100 feet.

Length

This is the length, in miles, of the route described. All figures are estimates, based on hiking the route and studying maps of the area. Note whether the distance is round trip or one way.

Time Needed

This is the time it will take to complete the described route. Because travel time varies tremendously from person to person, a range of time is given. Most hikers will fall into the middle of the time range. For example; if a time is listed as 1.5—4 hours, only a jogging pace will beat 1.5 hours, and 4 hours would be an easy stroll.

Difficulty

The difficulty ratings in this book refer to the skills needed to traverse a canyon rather than the amount of effort required. This is why in some cases, trips which might *seem* quite difficult are not rated any more difficult than a trip which *seems* quite easy. For instance, a trip down the Rainbow Bridge Trail through Cliff Canyon can be a grueling backpack trip. A hike into the Bill Williams River Canyon might seem pretty easy, yet both of these trips are rated moderate. So, what gives? Well, a hike to Rainbow Bridge is a long, rocky hike, but it is all on trail, and few skills are needed other than putting one foot in front of the other. The Bill Williams is much shorter and flatter, but there is a pool that you must either swim or climb around, requiring canyoneering skills other than just walking. Therefore, both of these hikes fall into the moderate category.

The only way to truly know what the difficulty ratings mean in this book is to go out and try them. Try an easy or moderate canyon first. If you find it challenging, think twice before attempting a more difficult canyon.

Different canyons with the same difficulty rating may present vastly different difficulties to you personally. For instance, you may not mind swimming a long frigid pool or finding your way through trailless country, but you may be scared to death of climbing. Next to the difficulty rating, there will be the specific canyoneering skills required listed in parentheses. Always read the trip description to get a better idea of what the canyon is like.

In general, this is what the different designations mean:

Easy: These canyons will usually have trails, but not always. There will never be any skills required for these canyons other than walking. This means no climbing, swimming, or route finding. There could be some elevation gain or loss, but most hikers could negotiate the route described by simply taking their time.

Moderate: Canyons listed as moderate may seem challenging to even an experienced hiker who is used to walking on trails, because often these canyons have no trails. However, you will find that moderate canyons do not require any skills beyond what an *average active person* would possess.

There will be no actual climbing, but you probably will have to use more than just your feet to get through the terrain. You may find yourself hopping between boulders or using your hands to lower yourself off a ledge. Scrambling will be necessary in most moderate canyons. Wading or swimming through pools might be needed, and basic route finding skills will often be required.

Difficult: Difficult canyons require canyoneering techniques that must be gained through experience. A difficult canyon will demand of you at least one of the following in a healthy dosage: climbing, swimming, or route finding. When comparing a difficult canyon with a moderate canyon, remember this: In a difficult canyon the pools are longer and colder, the exposure on climbs is greater, and the area is more remote.

Technical: A technical canyon will require at least one rappel, often in conjunction with swimming, climbing, and route finding.

Maps

There are basically two kinds of maps that are essential to exploring Arizona's canyons: topographical and forest service.

Topographical maps are quite accurate and essential to any extensive travel in the backcountry. However, topo maps take some time to learn how to read. Make sure you are comfortable reading a topo before trekking into the wilderness. Topos come in several scales, the most common and accurate being the 7.5 minute, or 1:24,000 series.

Forest service maps don't have terrain features on them like topos, but they do have roads and road numbers on them. Because of this, they are also a valuable resource. In general, the forest service map will help you get to the canyon, and the topo will show you how to get around once you're there.

There are two sub-headings under **Maps**. They are: **USGS** and **USFS**. These sub-headings stand for United States Geologic Survey and United States Forest Service, respectively. The USGS produces topographic maps, and the USFS publishes forest service maps. If there is no USFS sub-heading, there is no USFS map covering the area. The maps listed are the maps that cover the canyon being described. If a map is listed in parentheses, that means it covers a portion of the described route, but such a small portion that it probably isn't necessary.

Shuttle

In canyoneering, making a loop hike out of your journey is not always possible. Often the end of a canyoneering trip is nowhere near the place you started. In these cases, a shuttle will be necessary. This means you will need to drive two cars; one to leave at the lower end of the canyon for journey's end, and one to take you to the top of the canyon for the start of your trip. This can sometimes mean a ridiculous amount of driving, but there are some alternatives.

A mountain bike can be a great shuttle vehicle. Leave your bike at the finish of the hike, and cap your trip off with a bike ride back to your car. This can save you from bringing a second gas guzzling automobile. If a particular shuttle lends itself to bike riding, I will mention this under the shuttle heading. Of course, any roads that you can drive, you can ride, so technically any shuttle lends itself to bik-

A mountain bike shuttle

ing, but I've only mentioned mountain biking as an option if I consider it something that I would want to do. If you are a gnarly biker, feel free to pedal any shuttle.

Hitchhiking can work for some shuttles. Of course, hitchhiking is thought of as a dangerous activity by some people. It's true that you never know what kind of whacko might decide to pick you up. If you don't feel comfortable hitching, don't do it. However, sometimes hitchhiking proves to be an easy shuttle. For instance, the Pumphouse Wash hike finishes on highway 89A in Oak Creek Canyon, a popular tourist route. The flow of cars parading up this highway is a resource that can be easily tapped. I usually get a ride here with some retirees from Minnesota driving an immaculate white Cadillac. If you are thinking of hitching, consult the maps and make sure the roads you decide to hitchhike on are well travelled. I once spent a grueling eight hours walking under a hot desert sun in 85 degree heat because the road I had planned on hitchhiking had no traffic. My friend (whom I amazingly report is still my friend even after this incident) and I walked 15 miles along the dirt road before finally hitting a more major dirt road where, in the fading twilight, we frantically flagged down the first car to pass.

Some shuttles are short enough so that walking or jogging back to your vehicle is a good option. Of course, the slickest way to do a shuttle is to have a shuttle driver, someone who will drive your vehicle from point A to point B while you are exploring the canyon.

Under the shuttle heading, it will either say Yes, No, or Optional. If it says Yes, a shuttle is necessary to complete the trip as it is described. If I feel biking or walking the shuttle is a good option, I will mention it. If it says No, a shuttle is not needed. The route is either an out and back, or a loop, letting you finish exactly where you started. If it says Optional, a shuttle would be nice, but isn't necessary.

Access

These are directions to the canyon. Most of the time, mileages were taken from my truck's odometer. When I use the word <u>about</u>, mileages are not exact. "Follow this to its end, *about* another 4 miles." Under the subheading **Upper end** are the directions to the upstream end of the canyon. **Lower end** gives the directions to the downstream end of the canyon. A good map used in conjunction with the directions in this book will help you find your way.

Permits

Many of Arizona's canyons require permits for visitation. Basically, permits are needed for any hiking on reservation land, and for certain high-use canyons. Permits are instituted for a reason (sometimes a good one), and they should not be taken lightly. Stiff fines and other penalties have been levied on people who ignore permits, especially on reservation lands.

If exploration of a canyon requires a permit, a heading titled **Permits** will be listed below the maps heading. Under the permits heading, basic information on obtaining the necessary permit will be provided.

Trip Description

This is the meat of the guidebook. In the trip description, you will get a more thorough idea of what the canyon is like. I haven't taken you around every bend of every canyon in this guidebook, but I hope the trip description will let you know what you're getting into. My goal with the trip descriptions is to provide enough information so that you can confidently make the trip, but not so much information that you feel robbed of your sense of discovery. Every trip description was written first hand from my explorations. If there is any part of any route that I have not personally travelled, it will be mentioned as such in the text.

The Life Zones

The vegetation symbol at the bottom of every map indicates what life zone a canyon is in. This format was used in *The Arizona Rivers and Streams Guide*. I thought it was a helpful and easy-to-use format in that book, so I used it here.

The icons are only a general indication of a canyon's vegetation and life zone. Just because a saguaro icon is listed, it doesn't necessarily mean that you will find an actual saguaro cactus in that canyon. The icon is merely a representation of the life zone with which that canyon is most closely associated.

🌵 A **saguaro symbol** indicates the **Lower Sonoran zone**. This zone is found below 4,000' feet elevation. This is the life zone both Phoenix and Tucson are in. High temperatures and low rainfall force plants of the Lower Sonoran to make remarkable adaptations to their environment. The ocotillo sheds its leaves in times of drought. When the rain comes, it bursts out in a rich, deep green, with bright red flowers. Creosote bush has a waxy coating on the leaves that slows evaporation, thus saving water. Many cactus species are found here including: saguaro, barrel, Turk's head, hedgehog, prickly pear, and several types of cholla. Other plants dotting the Lower Sonoran landscape are nolina, Joshua tree, soaptree yucca, ocotillo, and creosote. Some trees in the Lower Sonoran are the paloverde, mesquite, and ironwood.

Lower Sonoran

🌿 The **juniper symbol** indicates the **Upper Sonoran zone**, from about 3,500' to 6,500'. In central Arizona, this zone is dominated by pinyon pine-juniper woodland. Extensive areas of chaparral are also found. In the north, plains of short grass steppe and a few scattered pinyons or junipers complete the scene. In southern Arizona, sweeping oak grasslands and chaparral make up the Upper Sonoran. Trees of the Upper Sonoran zone include alligator juniper, Utah juniper, one-seed juniper, Arizona cypress, Arizona white oak, Mexican blue oak, and pinyon pine. Contributing to the chaparral community of the Upper Sonoran is manzanita, scrub oak, barberry, and Apache plume.

Upper Sonoran

🔺 The **conifer symbol** represents the **Transition and Canadian zones**. The Transition zone runs from 6,000' to 8,000' feet, and the Canadian from 7,500' to 10,500' in Arizona. However, in canyon bottoms, these zones can be found at much lower elevations. The Transition zone is typically ponderosa pine forest. Rocky Mountain juniper and Gambel oak are also plentiful in the transition zone. Douglas fir, white fir, and aspen show up toward the upper end of the Transition. These same three species are widespread in the Canadian zone, along with Englemann spruce, Southwestern white pine, and corkbark fir.

Transition   Canadian

THE COLORADO PLATEAU

BUCKSKIN GULCH

General Description: Probably the premier slot canyon in the world
Best Season: June (You'll want hot weather, but no thunderstorms. Trips could be made in the upper end above the pools just about anytime.)
Elevation: 4,900'—4,100'
Length: 20 miles
Time Needed: 2—3 days
Difficulty: Moderate—Difficult (wading, possible swimming, one easy downclimb with steps)
Shuttle: Yes
Maps: USGS: Pine Hollow Canyon 7.5, West Clark Bench 7.5, Bridger Pt. 7.5
Permits: A reservation and permit are required for Buckskin Gulch and the Paria. Contact the B.L.M. in Kanab, Utah at (435) 688-2320.

Access: For the lower end of Buckskin and the Paria River trailhead, take highway 89 west out of Page about 30 miles. Between mileposts 20 and 21, turn south onto a dirt road with the Paria Ranger Station next to it. This is just east of where highway 89 crosses the Paria River. Continue south on this dirt road about 2 miles to the Whitehouse Ruins trailhead.

For the upper end of Buckskin, go about 35 miles west of Page and take the House Rock Valley Road south off highway 89. This is just west of milepost 26 and the cockscomb; a steep ridge of sandstone protruding from the desert. Head down House Rock Valley Road about 6 miles to the Wire Pass trailhead.

Trip Description: After leaving a shuttle vehicle near the normally dry Paria River at the Whitehouse Ruins trailhead, go to the Wire Pass trailhead to begin your hike into Buckskin.

Your route leads down the creekbed of Buckskin Gulch. This is a dark, narrow slot for most of its length. The route promises to be at least a little muddy and possibly quite wet. I have read reports of only encountering "occasional" pools in Buckskin, but when I was there, (October 1990, following a rainy September) there were lots of cold, muddy, deep pools. If you get a reliable report that the canyon is mostly dry, Buckskin Gulch could be hikeable even into winter, but with the conditions I found, I only recommend traversing Buckskin in hot weather. Don't go if there is a chance of rain. This is one of the few canyons where finding high ground in a flash flood would often be impossible. The canyon walls are sometimes less than 5 feet apart, and rarely more than 25 feet apart. There is one place to get out of the canyon, about halfway between Wire Pass and the Paria. It is a slope of sand and rock, which comes in from the north side of the canyon.

There is one fall in the canyon. It is about 1.5 miles above the Paria. It seems to be easily negotiated, with steps cut into the rock, but I have not seen it, or the lower 4 miles of Buckskin. Before reaching the falls, my party retreated to the sunny desert above after one and a half days of wading through the cold dark slot.

When you reach the Paria, hang a left and walk upstream about 7 miles to the Whitehouse Ruins trailhead.

Wading through Buckskin Gulch

BUCKSKIN GULCH

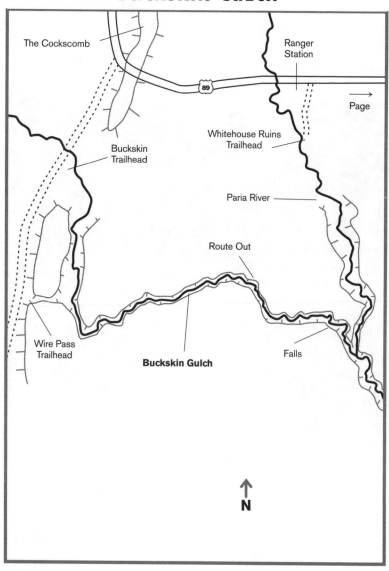

The Cockscomb

Ranger
Station

89

→
Page

Whitehouse Ruins
Trailhead

Buckskin
Trailhead

Paria River

Route Out

Wire Pass
Trailhead

Falls

Buckskin Gulch

↑
N

1 mile

main canyon bottom	
side canyon bottom	
trail	- - - - - - - - -
route	....
paved road	═══════════
dirt road	- - - - - - - - -

○ ♂ ⊗
tank spring guage

Lisa Gelczis

Spacing out in Buckskin

PARIA CANYON

General Description: A multi-day hike through one of the Colorado
Plateau's classic canyons
Best Season: April, May, mid-September to mid-November. Avoid thun-
derstorm season due to the flash flood danger. June would be hot.
Winter could be nice, but chilly.
Elevation: 4,280'—3,200'
Length: 42 miles
Hiking Time: 3—5 days
Difficulty: Easy
Shuttle: Yes. This is a long highway shuttle, but not that bad for a 4 day
hike.
Maps: USGS: Lees Ferry 1:62,500, Wrather Arch 7.5, Water Pockets 7.5,
Bridger Pt. 7.5, West Clark Bench 7.5, Ferry Swale 7.5
Permits: Obtain reservations and permits through the B.L.M. in Kanab, UT
at (435) 688-2320.

Access: Upper end: Take highway 89 west out of Page about 30 miles.
Between mileposts 20 and 21, turn south onto a dirt road with the Paria
Ranger station next to it. This is just east of where highway 89 crosses the
Paria River. Continue south on this dirt road about 2 miles to the
Whitehouse Ruins trailhead.
  Lower end: Take highway 89A from Bitter Springs toward Jacob Lake.
After crossing the Colorado River, turn right at the Marble Canyon Store
and follow the road to Lees Ferry. There is a trailhead and parking area at
Lees Ferry.

Trip Description: Paria Canyon is your classic Colorado Plateau canyon.
Huge sandstone walls streaked in desert varnish tower overhead, while
seeps of water trickle out of fern covered cracks in the walls. Paria Canyon
is an excellent representative of the many tributaries of Glen Canyon, most
of which are now under Lake Powell. It is a popular and well-documented
canyon. In fact, there is an entire book written on the Paria River and its
tributaries. See Kelsey's *Hiking and Exploring the Paria River.*
  Beginning at the Whitehouse Ruins trailhead, your route will lead
down the usually dry riverbed of the Paria. Underfoot is often gravel or
mud, making easy walking down most of the length of the Paria. There are
some narrows about 4 miles down from the trailhead. These narrows are
typical of Navajo sandstone slot canyons. Walls twist upward from the
shadowy depths, revealing a narrow strip of sky overhead. The narrows
begin to open slightly at about 7 miles, where Buckskin Gulch comes in on
the right. There are a few campsites here.
  Not far below Buckskin, the Paria normally develops a small flow as
springs feed the creek. Your route will demand that you cross the stream
numerous times, but it is rarely even knee deep. About 2 miles below

Buckskin, the narrows end. There are many nice campsites and several springs along much of Paria Canyon below here. Most of the springs are on river right. There are also springs in Wrather Canyon, at about mile 18, and up Bush Head Canyon at about mile 25. There are also arches, alcoves, and ruins to explore. Enjoy.

When Bush Head Canyon enters on the right, the canyon really begins to open up. There is a trail which starts about 0.7 miles above Bush Head Canyon. Once below Bush Head Canyon, this trail winds through the desert on the slope well above the river, on river right. This trail leads past some old ranches, including John Lee's ranch, "The Lonely Dell." Lees backbone (a prominent sandstone ridge) will mark your destination, and soon you'll arrive at Lees Ferry.

Huge walls dwarf hikers in Paria Canyon

Lisa Gelczis

PARIA

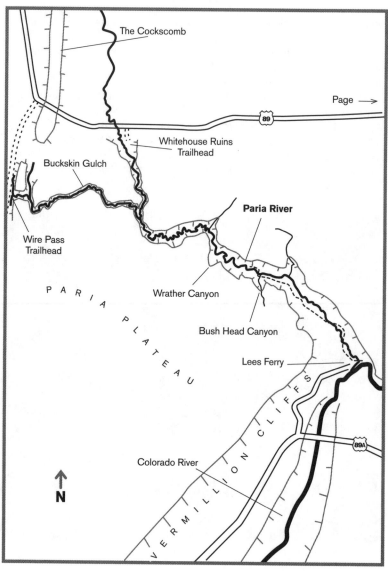

The Cockscomb

Page ⟶

89

Whitehouse Ruins
Trailhead

Buckskin Gulch

Paria River

Wire Pass
Trailhead

P A R I A   P L A T E A U

Wrather Canyon

Bush Head Canyon

Lees Ferry

89A

Colorado River

V E R M I L L I O N   C L I F F S

↑
N

1 mile

main canyon bottom
side canyon bottom
trail
route
paved road
dirt road

● ⚲ ⊗
tank spring guage

ANTELOPE CANYON

General Description: A famously photogenic sandstone slot
Best Season: October—November, March—June
Elevation: 4100'—4000'
Length: Up to a mile
Time Needed: 1—2 hours
Difficulty: Easy
Shuttle: No
Maps: Page 7.5, not that you'll need it
Permits: Tour fee is required. Call (520) 698-3360 for more information.

Access: Just out of Page, between town and the power plant on highway 98.

Trip Description: You've probably seen pictures of this canyon on a post-card or in *Arizona Highways* magazine. This is where all those photos of sun-lit sandstone walls come from.

The first thing you need to explore Antelope Canyon is your wallet. The impressive narrows and proximity to Page have made this canyon a tourist attraction. For $17 a head (as of June 1998) a Navajo guide will drive you to the canyon and escort you in to where you can get your very own post-card photo. To find out more, drive to the canyon and read the signs, or call (520) 638-3360.

Note: In August 1997, a deadly flash flood ripped through this canyon, killing 11 of the 12 people that were in the canyon at the time. This tragedy serves as a reminder that entering narrow canyons is always a gamble during the summer thunderstorm season.

Antelope Canyon is home to beautifully sculpted sandstone walls.

Lisa Gelczis

ANTELOPE CANYON

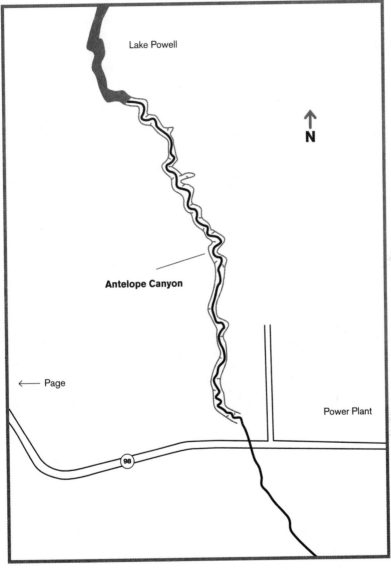

Lake Powell

N

Antelope Canyon

← Page

Power Plant

98

main canyon bottom	———————
side canyon bottom	———————
trail	- - - - - - - - - -
route	·················
paved road	═══════════
dirt road	: : : : : : : : : : :

● tank   ○́ spring   ⊗ guage

1 mile

CLIFF CANYON - RAINBOW BRIDGE

General Description: A trail hike into some of the world's finest sandstone canyon country
Best Season: October, November, April, May
Elevation: 6,360'—3,700'
Length: 13 miles from Rainbow Lodge to Rainbow Bridge
Time Needed: 2 or 3 days; if you are in good shape you could make it to the bridge and back in a very long day: 10—13 hours.
Difficulty: Easy—Moderate (a long trail with a 2,600-foot elevation change)
Shuttle: No
Maps: USGS: Rainbow Bridge 7.5, Chayahi Flat 7.5
Permits: Navajo Reservation permit, obtain at the visitor center/ranger station at the junction of highways 89 and 64 in Cameron. You can also get this permit at the Parks and Recreation Department in Window Rock. Call (520) 679-2303 for more information.

Access: Take highway 160 northeast out of Tuba City to highway 98. Head east/northeast on 98 for 12.3 miles and turn north on road 16, Navajo Mountain Road. Road 16 is paved at first but then turns to sand. From the intersection of highway 98 and road 16, follow road 16 for 32 miles to a major junction. Take the middle fork at this 3 way junction, toward Rainbow Bridge. Continue 4.8 more miles and take a right at the fork. In another 0.2 miles stay left at a fork, then bear left again in another 0.2 miles. The parking spot is 0.3 miles further, on the right, near a stone well. Don't leave anything valuable in your car here, or it will get ripped off! High clearance 2-wheel drives or 4-wheel drives can make it another mile up the road to the actual trailhead near the ruins of the Rainbow Lodge.

Trip Description: This hike is different from most in this book because you won't be travelling down a specific canyon. However, this classic trail would be a glaring omission from an Arizona canyoneering guide. The route described offers views and access into some of the most enchanting sandstone canyon country anywhere.

If you've parked at the well, follow the rocky road which gradually climbs the slope towards the base of Navajo Mountain. In about a mile, you'll arrive at the ruins of the Rainbow Lodge. Follow the trail and cairns from this point on. The trail will cross a few canyons while staying on the flanks of Navajo Mountain. The views in this stretch are awesome, spanning miles and miles of the sandstone wilderness below.

About 5 miles from the end of the road, the trail goes through a notch in the rocks called Yabut Pass, and makes a healthy 1,600 foot descent to the bottom of Cliff Canyon. About 2 miles down Cliff Canyon, a modest trickle springs up, providing the first water of the trip. There are a few campsites in Cliff Canyon as well. After staying in the bottom of Cliff

Canyon for a couple of miles, the trail makes a sharp turn to the northeast and pierces a slot in the sandstone called Redbud Pass. From here, you'll meander down Bridge Canyon with its clear stream and beautiful over-hanging walls of Navajo sandstone. Finally, Rainbow Bridge is visible and beneath it is, as Ed Abbey said, "Lake Powell: storage pond, silt trap, evap-oration tank and garbage dispose-all, a 180-mile-long national sewage lagoon."

Lisa Gelczis

The trail to Rainbow Bridge offers views of spectacular canyon country.

CLIFF CANYON - RAINBOW BRIDGE

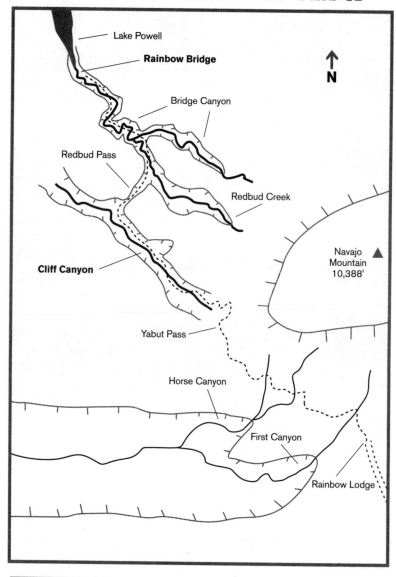

Lake Powell

Rainbow Bridge

N

Bridge Canyon

Redbud Pass

Redbud Creek

Cliff Canyon

Navajo
Mountain
10,388'

Yabut Pass

Horse Canyon

First Canyon

Rainbow Lodge

1 mile

main canyon bottom	———
side canyon bottom	———
trail	- - - - - -
route	··········
paved road	═══
dirt road	=======

● ♂ ⊗
tank spring guage

Lisa Gelczis

Rainbow Bridge

WATER HOLES CANYON

General Description: A narrow sandstone slot near Page
Best Season: October—June
Elevation: 4,600'—4,200'
Length: 2—4 miles
Time Needed: 1—4 hours
Difficulty: Moderate—Difficult (scrambling, climbing, possible wading)
Shuttle: No
Maps: USGS: Lees Ferry 1:62,500
Permits: Tour fee is required. Call (520) 698-3360 for more information.

Access: Highway 89 crosses over Water Holes Canyon about 5 miles south of Page. Park near the bridge.

Trip Description: Water Holes is a great little spot to see tight sandstone narrows right off the highway. You can walk upstream of the bridge or downstream. Both directions have narrows, but upstream is easier.

Heading upstream from the highway, there is a route into the canyon on the north side, about 50 yards from the bridge. Once in the sandy canyon bottom, there are nice narrows right away, then as you continue upstream, the canyon widens. At about 0.7 miles from the highway, a second set of narrows begins with tight, convoluted walls. There may be some muddy pools in here, but they are usually less than a foot deep. These narrows end with a sandstone slide, blocking any further progress without a significant climb.

Downstream of the bridge, there are more photogenic narrows, but access is blocked by an old car wedged between the walls, creating a fall. Unless you want to downclimb rusty metal, you'll have to exit the canyon and re-enter via a new route. There is a route about 20 yards downstream of the bridge, on the north side, which has a short 5.0 climb at the bottom. There are several other routes below here, both on the north and south sides.

There is a 15-foot fall a few hundred yards downstream of the highway that often has a rope in it. If you choose to descend this fall (don't trust the rope), your reward is another mile of canyon. Below this 15-foot fall, the canyon alternates between open and narrow until reaching a 30-foot fall—the turnaround point. Rather than climbing back up the 15-foot falls, I recommend finding a route out of the canyon, (there are several) and walking back to the highway across the desert.

The 30-foot fall is the first major drop of Lower Water Holes Canyon. To descend Lower Water Holes, you must complete several huge rappels into Glen Canyon, and have a boat shuttle at the bottom.

Lisa Gelczis

Holding up the walls in Water Holes

WATER HOLES

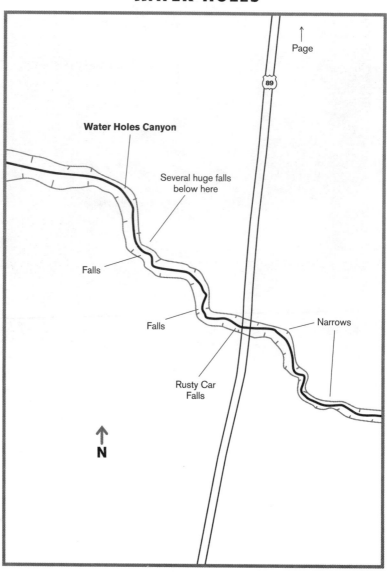

Page

89

Water Holes Canyon

Several huge falls
below here

Falls

Falls

Narrows

Rusty Car
Falls

N

1 mile

main canyon bottom	———
side canyon bottom	———
trail	- - - - - - -
route	··············
paved road	═══════
dirt road	┅┅┅┅┅

tank spring guage

Lisa Gelczis

Narrows in Water Holes Canyon

JACKASS CREEK

General Description: A short, scenic canyon within Marble Gorge
Best Season: October, November, February, March, April
Elevation: 3,900'—3,100'
Length: 5.5 miles round trip
Time Needed: 3—6 hours to river and back
Difficulty: Moderate (one downclimb with rope)
Shuttle: No
Maps: USGS: Glen Canyon Dam 1:100,000 / Bitter Springs 7.5
Permits: Obtain a Navajo hiking permit at the visitor center/ranger station in Cameron at the junction of highways 89 and 64. Call (520) 679-2303 for more information.

Access: Take highway 89A north from Bitter Springs toward Marble Canyon. Park near the bridge that spans the dry creekbed of Jackass Creek, between mile markers 532 and 531. There seems to be an additional parking area on the west side of the road near milepost 531.

Hike Description: Jackass Creek is an excellent and popular route for those trying to get to the cold waters of the Colorado for its superb trout fishing. It is the first major side canyon one comes to as they travel downstream through Marble Gorge. I have witnessed some large groups in this area who tend to trash the place. Please help keep it clean on your visit.

This canyon begins as a sandy wash beneath the highway, but cliff walls form almost instantly. On your way to the river, you will encounter some beautiful narrows and probably a little water in the creekbed. There is one fall of about 30 feet that is slick with moisture. There is usually a host of ropes at this fall to assist in your descent, but you should bring your own in case the ropes are not there. They have been known to disappear from time to time. Without a rope, the falls are a 5.1 downclimb.

Below the falls, some scrambling around house-sized boulders will soon have you at the river. The rapid here is called Badger Creek. It is the first rapid river runners encounter on their journey through the Grand Canyon.

A crude rappel at the falls in Jackass Creek Canyon. It is recommended that you lower your pack down falls before descending.

JACKASS CREEK

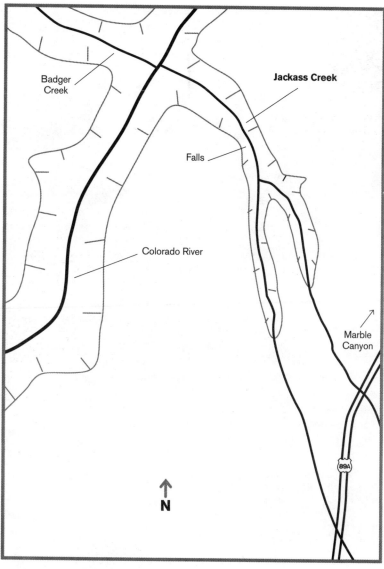

Badger Creek

Jackass Creek

Falls

Colorado River

Marble Canyon

89A

N

1 mile

main canyon bottom	
side canyon bottom	
trail	- - - - - - - - -
route	···························
paved road	═══════
dirt road	- - - - - - - -

● tank   ♂ spring   ⊗ guage

Standing next to a house-sized boulder in Jackass Creek

SOAP CREEK

General Description: A relatively quick access route to Marble Gorge and the Colorado River
Best Season: October—April
Elevation: 4100'—3120'
Length: 5 miles to river and back
Hiking Time: 3.5—6 hours
Difficulty: Moderate (scrambling)
Shuttle: No
Maps: USGS: Glen Canyon Dam 1:100,000, Bitter Springs 7.5

Access: Take highway 89A from Marble Canyon, AZ towards Jacob Lake. At 0.2 miles past mile marker 548, turn east onto a dirt road and follow it through a gate. Follow the B.L.M. signs another 0.6 miles to the trailhead.

Trip Description: This canyon begins as a sandy wash, but soon you'll find yourself scrambling through house-sized boulders in your descent to the mighty Colorado. Cairns lead to routes around a couple of steep sections. You might have to do some scrambling once or twice, but nothing too major. My dog made it down.

At the bottom, there is some nice sand and Soap Creek Rapids, a great place to relax and enjoy the depths of Marble Canyon.

Lisa Gelczis

Soap Creek empties into the Colorado River within Marble Canyon.

SOAP CREEK

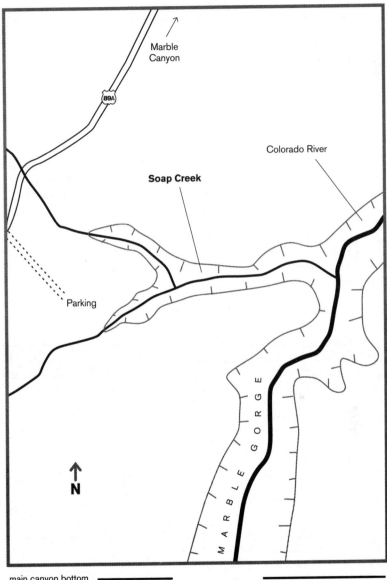

Marble
Canyon

89A

Colorado River

Soap Creek

Parking

MARBLE GORGE

N

main canyon bottom	————
side canyon bottom	———
trail	- - - - - - - -
route	·················
paved road	=====
dirt road	-------

1 mile

● ♂ ⊗
tank spring guage

RIDER CANYON

General Description: An isolated route into Marble Gorge
Best Season: October, November, March, April
Elevation: 4,500′—3,100′
Length: 5.5 miles round trip to the river
Time Needed: 1 or 2 days, 5 hours minimum for strong hikers
Difficulty: Moderate—Difficult (route finding, wading and climbing)
Shuttle: No
Maps: USGS: Glen Canyon Dam 1:100,000 metric
Permits: A Grand Canyon National Park backcountry permit is required if you are camping at the river.

Access: Finding this canyon beneath the non-descript rolling steppe of House Rock Valley can be as challenging as the hike itself. There are numerous dirt roads in the area, making wrong turn potential high. Hopefully, the advice given here will get you near the canyon, and your route finding instincts will get you in.

Take highway 89A between Marble Canyon and Jacob Lake. Just to the west of milepost 557, there is a dirt road heading south. Follow this dirt road. In 2.3 miles, bear left at a cattleguard. At 3.5 miles from the highway, stay left again. You will pass a ranch 4.8 miles from 89A. At 5.7 miles from the pavement, again stay left at a fork. At 11.9 miles, there is a hiker's sign directing you left. Go left here, then bear right at the next decent dirt road going in that direction. The route into the canyon is downstream of an old stock tank by about a mile. Cracks in the Kaibab limestone form the route.

If you were lucky, you drove right to the top of the route and spotted cairns marking the way in. If you were like me, and got frustrated with driving around in the desert, you can walk along the rim of Rider until finding the cairn-marked route.

Trip Description: Rider Canyon is possibly the most scenic, and certainly the most remote, of the Marble Gorge side canyons in this book. Once in the canyon bottom, falls and pools present route difficulties. At the mouth of the canyon, a wonderful beach accompanies House Rock Rapids, one of the larger drops along this section of the Colorado.

Assuming you were able to find the route, carefully make your way down through the Kaibab limestone. It is a steep path all the way to the bottom. Check your landmarks and place a cairn in the creekbed when you reach the bottom. Without a cairn, it would be easy to walk right by this route on your way back up the canyon.

In the canyon bottom, the footing alternates between big boulders and sandstone sidewalks. There are often potholes in here, but they dry up in summer. As the Supai sandstone closes in on the canyon, pools sit between narrow canyon walls. With some scrambling, you can keep your feet dry at every pool but one. There is one fall that requires either a 5.1 downclimb on the left with 20 feet of exposure, or a 15-foot rappel.

At the mouth of the canyon, the Colorado River can provide a bracing dip. If you brought your fishing pole and license, the rainbow trout are plentiful.

Staying dry in Rider Canyon

RIDER CANYON

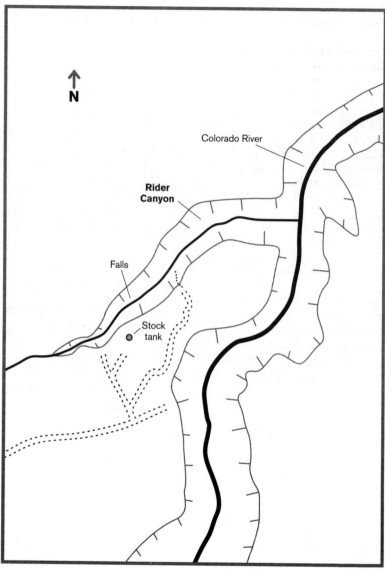

Colorado River

**Rider
Canyon**

Falls

Stock
tank

1 mile

main canyon bottom	▬▬▬
side canyon bottom	───
trail	- - - - - -
route	··············
paved road	═══
dirt road	⁝⁝⁝⁝⁝

● ⚲ ⊗
tank spring guage

TANNER AND HOT NA NAA WASHES

General Description: A 2 day backpack through the awesome Marble Gorge
Best Season: October—April
Elevation: 5,000'—3,100'
Length: 14 miles
Time Needed: 2 days. A fit hiker in a hurry could do it in a long day: 10 or 11 hours.
Difficulty: Moderate (route finding, scrambling)
Shuttle: No
Maps: USGS: Glen Canyon Dam 1:100,000/Bitter Springs 7.5
Permits: For hiking on Navajo land, get permits at the ranger station in Cameron at the junction of highways 89 and 64. Call (520) 698-2303 for more information.

Access: Park at Bitter Springs, near the junction of highways 89 and 89A between Page, Flagstaff, and Marble Canyon.

Trip Description: Tanner Wash is the canyon visible just to the west of Bitter Springs. The first part of this hike is relatively flat, going down the sandy wash between cliffs of Kaibab limestone. In a couple of miles, you'll enter the Coconino sandstone. Here, the canyon begins to drop more steeply and gets narrower. There is a 60 foot falls in this section, along with a few shallow pools. To get around the falls, head back upstream about 200 yards and get on the slope to the left, or south, above the Coconino sandstone cliff. Continue downstream about 0.5 miles, and descend back to the canyon bottom on the big colluvial slope. It's a steep descent, but no climbing is needed. Towards the bottom end of Tanner Wash, there are some neat narrows and small pools. This is your last chance at water, so stock up. You can't get to the river from Tanner Wash. At the mouth of Tanner, the Colorado River enters Sheer Wall Rapid. It lives up to its name.

   To get to Hot Na Naa Canyon, walk downstream along the Colorado (you will be about 300 feet above the river) on the Esplanade—the top of the Supai group formation. It's about 2 miles of flat but rocky walking from Tanner to Hot Na Naa. Hot Na Naa also cliffs out near the river, so don't plan on getting to the Colorado here. After wet weather, there may be some potholes in Hot Na Naa, but there is no permanent water. Walking up Hot Na Naa, you may have to scramble through some big boulders, but there are no real problem spots. Once in the upper reaches of Hot Na Naa, route finding skills will be necessary as you walk cross-country to the east to get back to Bitter Springs.

TANNER AND HOT NA NAA

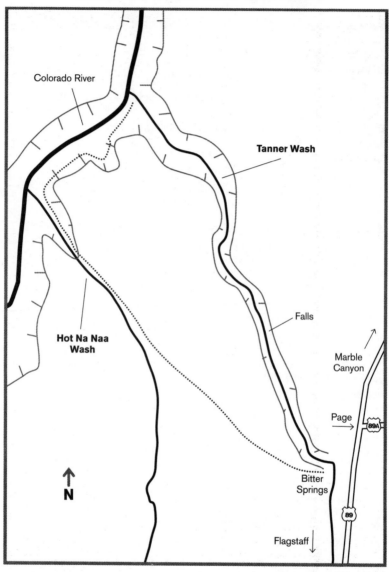

Colorado River

Tanner Wash

Falls

Hot Na Naa Wash

Marble Canyon

Page   89A

Bitter Springs

↑ N

Flagstaff ↓

89

1 mile

main canyon bottom	▬▬▬▬
side canyon bottom	————
trail	- - - - -
route	··········
paved road	═══════
dirt road	≡≡≡≡≡≡

● tank   ♂ spring   ⊗ guage

Narrows at the mouth of Tanner Wash

LITTLE COLORADO RIVER GORGE
Blue Spring

General Description: A steep route into an incredible gorge
Best Season: March—May, late September—November. Foot travel in this gorge should only be attempted when the river is very low or altogether dry.
Elevation: 5,300'—3,160'
Length: 1 mile to Blue Spring
Time Needed: 2 days, or 4—8 hours to go down and back out in 1 day.
Difficulty: Difficult (climbing)
Shuttle: No
Maps: USGS: Blue Spring 7.5
Permits: Navajo reservation permit. Obtain in Cameron at the visitor center/ranger station at the junction of highways 89 and 64. Call (520) 679-2303 for more information.

Access: From Cameron, take highway 64 west into Grand Canyon National Park. The road you want is about 50 yards beyond the Desert View entrance station. Unless you can sweet-talk the entrance guard, you'll have to pay the $20 entrance fee to the park. Once past the entrance station, turn right onto Cape Solitude Road. This road is steep, rocky, and can be muddy. It requires a four-wheel drive and some off-road driving skill!
In 1 mile down Cape Solitude Road, stay to the left. The right fork leads to a sewage lagoon. At 3.4 miles from highway 64, bear left. At 9.0 miles stay straight. At 12.4 miles, stay left. At 13.3 miles, bear left. At 13.9 miles, take a deep breath, you've made it.
Your destination is a point on the rim of the gorge just west of Gold Hill. Don't confuse Gold Hill with Cedar Mountain. Cedar Mountain is the most prominent butte in the area, and it is covered with juniper trees. Gold Hill is much smaller, nearly void of trees and closer to the rim of the gorge. Both Gold Hill and Cedar Mountain are visible from highway 64, many miles before the entrance to the park.

Trip Description: Before setting out on this trip, check on the current flow of the Little Colorado River at Cameron. If it is more than 50 cubic feet per second, don't go. Crossing the river will be hazardous, and the lovely blue water of Blue Spring will be drowned out by the chocolate brown water of the main river. Ideal conditions are when the Little Colorado is dry or just a trickle, like less than 10 c.f.s. You can make a quick scan of the flow below the bridge in Cameron. If it is anything more than a little creek here, it is too high.
This steep route leads into the impressive Little Colorado River Gorge at Blue Spring, the source of the Little Colorado's azure blue flow. With binoculars, you should be able to spot the spring from the canyon rim. The

route begins just east of the parking spot. On the map, it is to the northwest, or just downstream, of Blue Spring. Cairns will lead you all the way down through cliffs of Kaibab limestone and Coconino sandstone, then across a bench of Hermit shale. The final cliff just above the river is Redwall limestone. To get through this layer, the route leads upstream about 200 yards before descending a short, moderate slope to the river.

If you're an acrophobiac (fear of high places), this trip isn't for you. There are a couple of spots along this route where you may want to shed your pack to downclimb. The climbs are mostly grade 4 scrambles, with one or two spots bordering on 5th class climbing. The exposure on some of the scrambles is huge. Up to 200 feet of air hangs beneath your toes in places. All the moves with big exposure, though, are class 4. If you are comfortable around high places, there should be no problems, but if you are uneasy around heights, this will be challenging.

Once at the bottom, you can enjoy beaches of sand and Blue Spring—an outlet for a large portion of northern Arizona's subterranean water. It gushes out of the river left bank of Redwall limestone with a Caribbean-like turquoise blue color. The temperature of the water nearly emulates the tropics too, it is over 70 degrees fahrenheit. The combination of warm, clear water and a deep gorge make this spot an Eden.

Downstream, more springs add to the river's flow and canyoneers can expect lots of swimming and wading. I have only explored 1 mile below the springs, and I had to swim once in that stretch. It is about 12 miles to the Colorado River from Blue Spring. If you go that far, you technically need a permit from the park.

My upstream progress is even less impressive than my downstream. I was turned back in 0.5 miles by quicksand. There is supposedly quicksand in the Little Colorado Gorge, and though I can't imagine it's as lethal as the maiden-sucking stuff we see in the movies, the squishy thigh deep mud I encountered was intimidating enough to turn me back. Progress could safely be made through here if two people crossed pools separately and carried a rope. It would definitely be a muddy experience.

The real problem with exploring this gorge upstream of Blue Spring is timing. Ideal conditions are found only after a prolonged dry spell, and finding good water could be a problem then. Your best chances for exploring the Little Colorado Gorge would probably come in June (after spring runoff), October or early November (after monsoon season, but before winter sets in).

LITTLE COLORADO

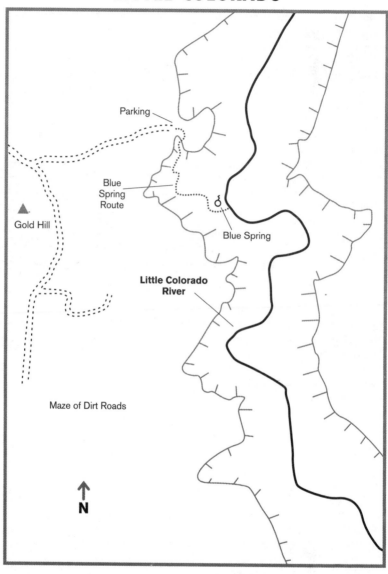

Parking

Blue
Spring
Route

Gold Hill

Blue Spring

**Little Colorado
River**

Maze of Dirt Roads

N

1 mile

main canyon bottom	
side canyon bottom	
trail	
route	
paved road	
dirt road	

tank spring guage

Big exposure on the Blue Spring route.

DIAMOND CREEK

General Description: A narrow canyon with a running stream in western Grand Canyon
Best Season: October—April
Elevation: 2,100'—1,520'
Time Needed: 2—6 hours
Length: 7 miles round trip
Difficulty: Moderate (scrambling)
Shuttle: No
Maps: USGS: Diamond Peak 7.5, Peach Springs NE 7.5
Permits: A Hualapai Reservation hiking permit is required, obtain this in Peach Springs at the parks and recreation office.

Access: From Seligman, take route 66 west to Peach Springs. From Peach Springs, take the Diamond Creek Road for 18.8 miles to a parking spot just before the road crosses Diamond Creek.

Trip Description: From the parking area, head upstream along the creek. The narrows begin in about a mile. The creek twists and tumbles between smooth walls of metamorphic rock. There are a couple spots where you'll have to scramble up boulders, and your feet will likely get wet. Keep your eyes peeled for bighorn sheep, there are certainly lots in the area. When you reach the head of the narrows in about 3.5 miles, turn around and come back down the creek.

While in the area, you may want to follow the road down Diamond Creek a couple miles to the Colorado River. Here, at the mouth of Diamond Creek, is the first spot a Grand Canyon river trip can take out once leaving Lees Ferry 226 miles upriver.

DIAMOND CREEK

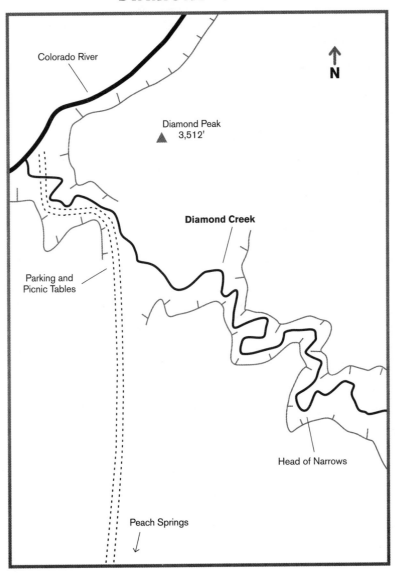

Colorado River

N

Diamond Peak
▲ 3,512'

Diamond Creek

Parking and
Picnic Tables

Head of Narrows

Peach Springs

main canyon bottom	——————
side canyon bottom	———
trail	- - - - - - - - -
route	··················
paved road	═══════
dirt road	: : : : : : : : :

1 mile

● tank   ♂ spring   ⊗ guage

WALNUT CANYON

General Description: A canyon with numerous ruins near Flagstaff
Best Season: All year except during heavy snows
Elevation: 6,700'—6,320'
Length: The Island Trail is 1 mile
Time Needed: 1—2 hours
Difficulty: Easy
Shuttle: No
Maps: USGS: Flagstaff East 7.5, USFS: Coconino N.F.

Access: Take I-40 east out of Flagstaff a few miles. Follow the signs to Walnut Canyon National Monument.

Trip Description: Walnut Canyon was home to the Sinaguans—the people of northern Arizona several hundred years ago. The national monument here protects the ruins those people left behind.

There is a paved trail to the bottom of the canyon with interpretive signs along the way. This trail is called the Island Trail, and it leads to some well preserved ruins.

Hiking up or downstream through the backcountry is prohibited by the park service, unless you get written permission from the park superintendent. Enjoy your national monument.

WALNUT CANYON

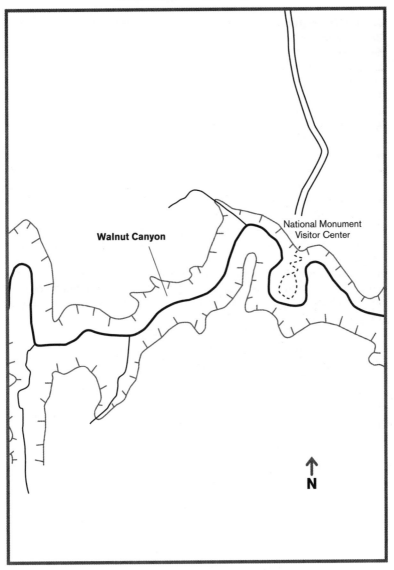

Walnut Canyon

National Monument
Visitor Center

N

main canyon bottom	
side canyon bottom	1 mile
trail	
route	
paved road	
dirt road	

tank spring guage

EAST CLEAR CREEK

General Description: A narrow, water-filled sandstone gorge.
Best Season: mid-May through June (hot weather, no thunderstorms)
Elevation: 5,000'—4,800'
Length: 1—4 miles one way
Time Needed: 1 hour—all day
Difficulty: Difficult (swimming, route finding)
Shuttle: No
Maps: USGS: Clear Creek Reservoir 7.5

Access: Take highway 87 south out of Winslow. About a mile south of town, turn east on route 99, following signs for McHood Park Lake. In 4.4 miles you will cross the Clear Creek Reservoir. Stay on 99, and at 0.3 miles past milepost 37, take a right onto a dirt road at some prominent sandstone rocks beside the highway. In 0.2 miles, stay left at a second group of rocks. Bear right at any other forks you come to. Park at a flat area where the road turns east along a small drainage. This is 0.7 miles from the highway.

Trip Description: This section of East Clear Creek is in a narrow sandstone gorge. It is not tremendously deep, but the canyon walls are quite sheer, making getting in and out of the canyon a problem. In fact, the route described here is the only one I found for 4 miles upstream of the reservoir. Flash floods could be lethal in here; be careful.

From the parking spot, walk down the side drainage to the south of the road, toward the gorge. When this drainage cliffs out above the reservoir, head upstream and cross a second side drainage. This one has a fence coming into it. Continue heading upstream, staying near the edge, and you should see the route into Clear Creek marked with cairns about 150 yards from the fenced side drainage. This route drops in just above where Clear Creek is usually swallowed by the reservoir.

In the canyon bottom, there is thick riparian vegetation (including poison ivy) along the stream. Exploring upstream, you will find a long deep pool about 0.2 miles from the route in. This pool must be swum to explore upstream further. If you choose to continue, you'll encounter several more deep pools filling the canyon bottom. This is a great place to splash around on a hot day. Check it out before monsoon season though, East Clear Creek is a big drainage. A torrential downpour could be raging in the high country along Clear Creek's headwaters while cloudless skies are overhead in these lower narrows. With the sheer walls in this section, a flash flood would have little trouble snatching your desperately clinging body from the edge of the gorge.

When you must, return downstream to the route from which you came. The truly adventurous may want to continue upstream. I have only seen the first 4 miles above the reservoir.

Exploring watery East Clear Creek

EAST CLEAR CREEK

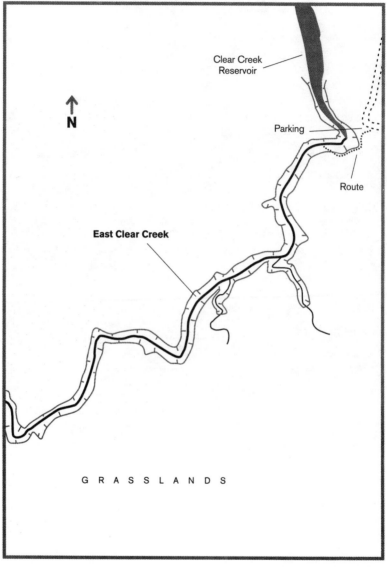

1 mile

main canyon bottom
side canyon bottom
trail
route
paved road
dirt road

tank spring guage

East Clear Creek gorge

CHEVELON CANYON

General Description: An open, forested canyon with a perennial stream
Best Season: mid-April through October
Elevation: 6,300'—6,100'
Length: 16 miles round trip from Chevelon Crossing to Chevelon Reservoir
Time Needed: From Chevelon Crossing to Chevelon Reservoir is 3.5—6 hours one way. To go to the lake and back in one day would be a full day: 7—12 hours. I recommend taking 2 days.
Difficulty: Easy
Shuttle: Optional. You could make this a one way hike by dropping a vehicle at either the reservoir or the crossing. It is described here as an out and back.
Maps: USGS: Chevelon Crossing 7.5, USFS: Apache Sitgreaves N.F.

Access: Take highway 99 south out of Winslow about 26 miles and make a left on road #504. Follow road #504 for 7.3 miles to Chevelon Crossing on Chevelon Creek. Park near here to start your journey upstream. If you want to drive a shuttle, go back up the hill to road #169 and take it south about 9 miles to #169B, then go down #169B about two miles to Chevelon Lake Campground.

Trip Description: When I reflect on the various canyons I've visited, different adjectives come to mind; deep, cold, dry, rugged. The first word that pops into my head when I hear Chevelon is: pleasant. There is nothing tremendously awe-inspiring here, but this babbling brook winding among parks of ponderosa pine and Gambel oak, beneath sunny slopes of pinyon pine and juniper can be blissfully serene.

There is an unmaintained trail that heads upstream from Chevelon Crossing. It will direct you across the creek a few times, but with some deft rock hopping, you should be able to keep your feet dry. Big pools on the creek house a healthy population of crawdads and fish. Trout fisherman have ample opportunity to test their skills here. Plenty of campsites can be found throughout this canyon.

The trail fades as you approach the dam which holds back Chevelon Reservoir. This earthen dam was constructed by the Fish and Game Department to provide a lake for fishing.

CHEVELON

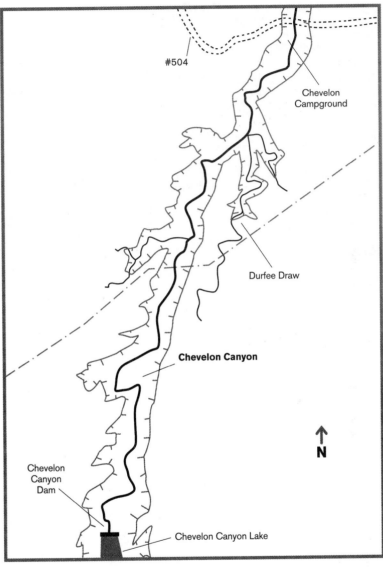

#504

Chevelon
Campground

Durfee Draw

Chevelon Canyon

↑
N

Chevelon
Canyon
Dam

Chevelon Canyon Lake

main canyon bottom	▬▬▬▬▬
side canyon bottom	▬▬▬▬▬
trail	- - - - - - - - -
route	··········
paved road	════════
dirt road	∷∷∷∷∷∷∷

●   ⚲   ⊗
tank spring guage

1 mile

Camping along Chevelon Creek.

THE MOGOLLON RIM

SYCAMORE CANYON

overview

Sycamore Canyon is a massive canyon gouging the northwestern portion of the Mogollon Rim. Its watershed extends to the flanks of the 12,000-foot high San Francisco Peaks. The canyon is several miles wide in places. It is often referred to as "The Little Grand Canyon."

To traverse all of Sycamore Canyon, from top to bottom, would take 4 or 5 days. Because of the enormity of this canyon, I have broken it down into 4 sections. Each section by itself is suitable for single-day or multi-day excursions. The four sections, as I have divided them, are as follows:

Headwaters: Sycamore Rim trail - Geronimo Spring
Upper Sycamore: Geronimo Spring - Taylor Cabin
Central Sycamore: Taylor Cabin - Parsons Spring
Lower Sycamore: Parsons Spring - Verde River

SYCAMORE CANYON

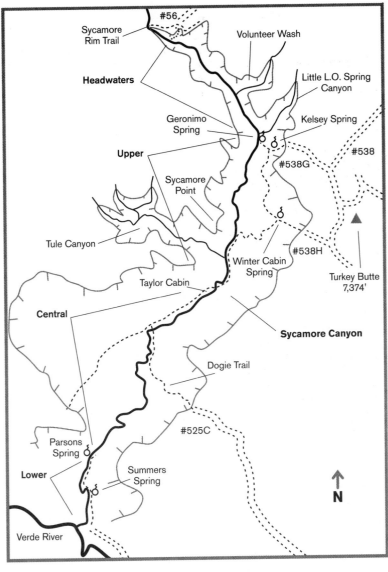

Sycamore Rim Trail

#56

Volunteer Wash

Headwaters

Little L.O. Spring Canyon

Geronimo Spring

Kelsey Spring

Upper

#538

#538G

Sycamore Point

#538H

Tule Canyon

Winter Cabin Spring

Turkey Butte 7,374'

Taylor Cabin

Sycamore Canyon

Central

Dogie Trail

#525C

Parsons Spring

Summers Spring

Lower

N

Verde River

main canyon bottom	————
side canyon bottom	———
trail	- - - - - -
route	··················
paved road	═══════
dirt road	┄┄┄┄┄

1 mile

tank   spring   guage

SYCAMORE CANYON
headwaters

General Description: A boulder hop through the little visited uppermost reaches of the Sycamore Canyon Wilderness
Best Season: April—October
Elevation: 6,640'—5,140'
Length: 8 miles one way
Time Needed: 3.5—7 hours from trailhead to trailhead
Difficulty: Moderate (boulder hopping, route finding)
Shuttle: Optional. A shuttle is necessary here unless you want to do an out-and-back hike. Given the length of this shuttle, an out-and-back hike might be a good option.
Maps: USGS: Bill Williams Mtn. 1:62,500, Sycamore Point 7.5, USFS: Coconino N.F., Kaibab N.F. south

Access: Lower end: For the Kelsey Spring trailhead, take Woody Mountain Road #231 south from route 66 in west Flagstaff for 12.1 miles. Turn right onto road #538. Follow #538 for 5.5 miles and go right onto #538G. The Kelsey Spring trailhead is 2 miles down road #538G. The last 0.5 miles is pretty rough, it may require a high clearance vehicle.

Upper end: For the Sycamore Rim trailhead, take I-40 west out of Flagstaff for about 15 miles to the Parks exit. Take road #141 south for about 9 miles. When road #141 makes a 90-degree turn to the <u>north</u>, stay straight, onto road #13. Follow road #13 for 0.9 miles and intersect road #56. Follow road #56 south to its end in 2.2 miles.

Trip Description: From the Sycamore Rim trailhead, the Sycamore Rim trail leads about 0.3 miles to, you guessed it, the rim of Sycamore Canyon. There is a steep drainage in the gray-black basaltic rock here that leads into the main Sycamore Canyon. Follow the bed of this basalt drainage down to the main canyon. You'll be hopping between car-sized boulders most of the way. There is a Douglas fir tree in this drainage that is quite possibly the largest of its species in Arizona.

When you get near the main canyon, the side drainage you're in will cliff out. To get into Sycamore, walk upstream, above the Kaibab limestone that guards the canyon bottom. After about 75 yards of clawing through chaparral, look for a gully leading down to the creekbed. A scramble down this gully provides access to the canyon bottom.

Once in the creekbed of Sycamore Canyon, it's rock hopping downstream for the next 5 miles to the Kelsey Spring trail. There are pretty cliff walls in the Kaibab limestone and some cool shady spots on the ponderosa pine and Douglas fir covered hillsides. Water in the creekbed will be a rare find, unless you are on the heels of plentiful rain or snow. The real attraction here is the solitude. Your likeliest companions in this canyon are the elk, bear, deer, cougars, coyotes, skunks, raccoons, squirrels, eagles, hawks, and turkey vultures that live here.

About 1.5 miles below the confluence with Volunteer Wash, keep your eyes peeled for a cairn directing you to a trail on creek left. This trail will lead to Geronimo Spring, possibly the first water you'll encounter on the trip. Geronimo Spring is home to a lovely lush campsite. It is located about 75 yards to the east of the Sycamore creekbed, at the mouth of Little L O Canyon.

The Kelsey Spring trail trudges relentlessly uphill from here, passing Babes Hole Spring and Kelsey Spring on the way to the rim and road #538G. The trail is steep most of the way, but it is easy to follow and passes some wonderful big ponderosas en route to the top. Both Babes Hole and Kelsey springs make pleasant rest spots.

Wilderness

SYCAMORE CANYON

upper

General Description: A remote section of canyon suitable for a long day
hike or a loop backpack route
Best Season: mid—March to November
Elevation: 6,640'—4,400'
Length: 9—12 miles. This section of creekbed, from Geronimo Spring to
Taylor Cabin, is 9 miles. To go down the Kelsey Spring trail, down-
stream along the creekbed, and out the Winter Cabin trail, is about
12 miles.
Hiking Time: 5—9 hours or 2 days
Difficulty: Moderate (boulder hopping)
Shuttle: Optional. It is an easy mountain bike shuttle from Winter Cabin
trailhead to Kelsey Spring trailhead.
Maps: USGS: Sycamore Pt. 7.5, Loy Butte 7.5, USFS: Coconino
N.F./Kaibab N.F.

Access: Upper trailhead: For the Kelsey Spring trailhead, take Woody
Mountain Road #231 south from route 66 in west Flagstaff for 12.1 miles.
Turn right onto road #538. Follow #538 for 5.5 miles and go right onto
#538G. The Kelsey Spring trailhead is 2 miles down road #538G. The last
0.5 miles is pretty rough and may require a high clearance vehicle.
  Lower trailhead: Take Woody Mountain Road #231 south from Route
66 in west Flagstaff for 12.1 miles. Turn right onto road #538. Follow
#538 for 8.9 miles and turn right towards Winter Cabin trailhead on road
#538H. Follow #538H 0.6 miles to the Winter Cabin trailhead.

Trip Description: The creekbed in this portion of Sycamore Canyon is tra-
versed even less than the headwaters stretch upstream. Additionally, this
remote section is home to the only narrows in Sycamore Canyon. A brief
alley of Coconino sandstone walls the creekbed here. As you descend the
creekbed from Geronimo Spring toward Taylor Cabin, Sycamore Canyon
undergoes an obvious change from a forested canyon in the high country
to an open canyon with red sandstone buttes poking out of the chaparral.
At higher elevations within this section of canyon, ponderosa pines shade
pleasant hiking trails.
  As you descend the Kelsey Spring trail, you will pass an intersection
with trail #3 to Dorsey Spring. This trail heads south, staying relatively
flat on its journey to Dorsey Spring and then Winter Cabin Spring, 4.5
miles distant. For enjoyable backpacking, this is the route to take. To
explore the canyon bottom, proceed down trail #6 to Geronimo Spring.
You'll pass some huge orange-barked ponderosa pines on the way down.
The last few hundred vertical feet of trail is a steep descent through a
pine/fir forest.

You'll be boulder hopping most of the way between Geronimo Spring and Taylor Cabin. The footing ranges from solid gray boulders to gravel bars of loosely-piled cobbles that frustratingly give way underfoot. There may be some small pools of water in the Coconino sandstone narrows, but unless you are here after a big snowmelt or rainstorm, the creekbed will be mostly or entirely dry. Taylor Cabin is a rock shelter built into the cliff on creek right about 9 miles down from Geronimo Spring. This marks the end of the Upper Sycamore section.

A nice loop can be made by using the Winter Cabin trail #70. Winter Cabin trail exits the canyon bottom nearly directly across from Sycamore Point, a promontory on the western rim of the canyon. Look for a cairn and a trail switchbacking uphill just north of a side drainage on creek left. Winter Cabin Trail makes a hot climb through chaparral before finally level-ing off in the ponderosas near Winter Cabin—a wonderful grassy spot next to a spring. From here, you may travel north on trail #3 toward Dorsey Spring, or climb one more mile out to the Winter Cabin trailhead.

The narrowest part of Sycamore Canyon is in this upper section.

SYCAMORE CANYON
central

General Description: A big canyon with wide open spaces and expansive
  views
Best Season: September—April
Elevation: 4,880'—3,760'
Length: 8 miles from Sycamore Pass to Taylor Cabin via the Dogie Trail. 12
  miles from Taylor Cabin to Parsons Spring along the creek.
Time Needed: 1—3 days
Difficulty: Easy—Moderate (long rocky trails, possible boulder hopping)
Shuttle: No
Maps: USGS: Loy Butte 7.5, (Sycamore Pt. 7.5), USFS: Coconino N.F.,
  Prescott N.F.

Access: Take highway 89A southwest out of Sedona about 6 miles and turn
north on road #525. Follow the signs to Sycamore Pass. At 2.7 miles from the
highway, stay left on #525C. In another 3.2 miles, stay right on #525C. In 5.2
more miles, you'll be at Sycamore Pass and the Dogie trailhead. Park here.

Trip Description: This part of Sycamore Canyon is probably the most popular for backpacking. Don't let its popularity fool you; this is wild country.
Sign of mountain lion is not uncommon.

The Dogie trail is the primary artery leading into this portion of the
wilderness. It descends from Sycamore Pass through a forest of juniper and
pinyon towards the creek, then parallels the creek, staying a couple hundred
feet above. Finally, the Dogie trail crosses the creekbed of Sycamore and
intersects trail #63 coming from the southwest. You'll be lucky if you have
seen any water at this point.

Trail #63 heads upstream, staying on a benchland well above the creek
on its way to Taylor Cabin. Taylor Cabin is a quaint little ranching cabin built
into an overhang of Supai sandstone. It could be a welcome shelter in foul
weather, but I wouldn't sleep in it otherwise, unless you enjoy being a dance
floor for mice. This can be an idyllic spot after a good winter, when the creek
is flowing. During dry spells, finding water can be a problem.

There is sometimes a trail along the creekbed, but it periodically gets
washed away by floods. Trail #63 is your best bet for easy walking. The
creekbed is wide, with sycamore trees scattered across a bed of loose river
cobble.

Some hikers make a loop in this section of canyon by continuing
upstream from Taylor Cabin, taking trail #35 up to Bunker Ridge, then following the powerlines across Casner Mtn. and back to Sycamore Pass.
Whatever trip you decide to make, this is big wild country to do it in.

Taylor Cabin is a popular destination in central Sycamore Canyon.

SYCAMORE CANYON
lower

General Description: A well-watered and green canyon, popular with those in search of a swimming hole
Best Season: All year
Elevation: 3,760'—3,560'
Length: 4 miles to Parsons Spring
Time Needed: 3.5 hours—all day
Difficulty: Easy
Shuttle: No
Maps: USGS: Clarkdale 7.5, USFS: Coconino N.F., Prescott N.F.

Access: From Cottonwood, follow the signs toward Tuzigoot National Monument. After turning right off highway 89A towards Tuzigoot, continue 0.5 miles and turn left onto a dirt road. This dirt road heads upstream along the Verde River for about 10.8 miles to the Sycamore Canyon trailhead.

Trip Description: The lower end of Sycamore Canyon is a much tamer place than the wilderness upstream. The main attraction here is clear water, lush greenery, and easy access, not rugged wilderness.

From the trailhead, a well-used trail gradually descends to the canyon bottom and creek in about a quarter mile. Sycamores, Arizona walnuts, and Fremont cottonwoods provide idyllic shady glens along this perennial stream.

Though there are lovely campsites in this lower stretch, camping is not allowed, because the impact is too great in this high use area. Thanks to the no camping rule, lower Sycamore is in much better shape today than it was a few years ago, when littered fire rings made the place a mess.

In a little over a mile from the trailhead, Summers Spring comes bubbling out of the ground in a crystal clear flow, giving life to numerous riparian plants such as cardinal flower and watercress.

Parsons Spring is four miles from the trailhead. About halfway to Parsons Spring, a popular swimming hole is tucked against a cliff on creek right. Parsons is also a nice swimming hole, though mineralization prevents it from being as clear as Summers Spring.

Big views can be found in Sycamore Canyon.

PUMPHOUSE WASH

General Description: A cool and shady canyon on the headwaters of famous Oak Creek
Best Season: May—November
Elevation: 6,400'—5,689'
Length: 3.5 miles one way
Time Needed: 2.5—6.5 hours one way
Difficulty: Moderate (boulder hopping, scrambling)
Shuttle: Optional
Maps: USGS: Mountainaire 7.5, USFS: Coconino N.F.

Access: Lower end: Drive south out of Flagstaff about 14 miles on highway 89A to the bottom of the switchbacks at the head of Oak Creek Canyon. Park near the bridge that crosses Pumphouse Wash.

Upper end: Drive back up the switchbacks. 1.5 miles north of the Oak Creek overlook, turn east onto road #237. This is about 10.5 miles south of Flagstaff, between mileposts 391 and 392. Follow road #237 down the hill to where it crosses Pumphouse Wash and park. You could save yourself about 0.4 miles of relatively unimpressive creekbed walking by parking about 0.4 miles up the road from the Pumphouse Wash crossing. From here it is a short bushwhack down to the creekbed.

Trip Description: Pumphouse Wash is essentially upper Oak Creek Canyon. Kelly and James canyons are major tributaries of Pumphouse. Between these three canyons, various route options are available to the canyoneer.

The Pumphouse hike starts as a boulder hop through a basalt-filled streambed. About 1.5 miles down from the road #237 crossing, there is a 14-foot falls in the basalt, with a pool below it. The scrambling route around this fall is on the left.

At 0.4 miles below the falls, James Canyon enters from the left, and it is here where things get more interesting. Sheer rock faces of Coconino sandstone appear, and the canyon deepens. Bigtooth maple and Douglas fir cover the slopes of the canyon, creating a lush backdrop for the uniquely-eroded sandstone. There could be some wading necessary in this canyon following a wet winter. Usually, there are just some scattered pools, easily avoided. There is one section of slot narrows, but they are incised in the riverbed, with a broad sandstone sidewalk above them. The slot is fun to peer into, but there is no need to actually travel through its cold dark pools. A mile below the slot, you'll arrive at highway 89A.

PUMPHOUSE / KELLY / JAMES

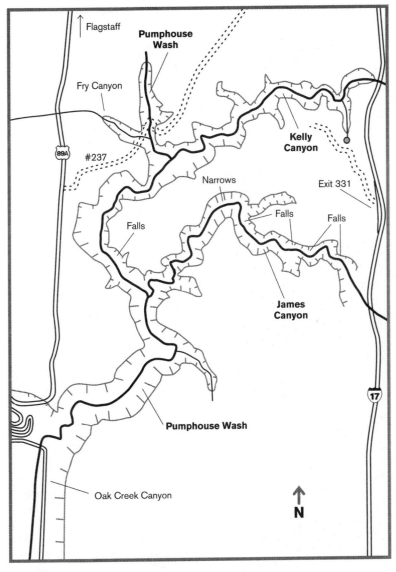

Flagstaff

Pumphouse
Wash

Fry Canyon

Kelly
Canyon

89A

#237

Narrows

Exit 331

Falls

Falls

Falls

Falls

James
Canyon

17

Pumphouse Wash

Oak Creek Canyon

N

main canyon bottom	————————
side canyon bottom	————
trail	- - - - - - - - -
route	·················
paved road	════════
dirt road	::::::::::::::::

1 mile

tank spring guage

Playing in the eroded sandstone of Pumphouse Wash

Pumphouse Wash at high water
Don't attempt to hike here when it looks like this.

KELLY CANYON

General Description: A forested canyon near Flagstaff
Best Season: April—November. Anytime there is no snow
Elevation: 6,700'—6,300'
Length: 3.5 miles with shuttle, 6 miles without shuttle
Time Needed: 1.5—3.5 hours with shuttle, 3—7 hours without shuttle.
Difficulty: Easy—Moderate (boulder hopping)
Shuttle: Optional
Maps: USGS: Mountainaire 7.5, USFS: Coconino N.F.

Access: Lower end: Drive south from Flagstaff on highway 89A about 10.5 miles to road #237. This is located between mileposts 391 and 392. Take road #237 down the hill to where it crosses Pumphouse Wash—about 1.4 miles. Park here.

Upper end: Take I-17 south from Flagstaff about 9 miles and take exit 331—Kelly Canyon Road. Follow Kelly Canyon Road for 0.5 miles and park near a large tank to the east of the road.

Trip Description: Of the three major headwater canyons of Oak Creek—James, Kelly, and Pumphouse—Kelly Canyon is the easiest. There is a game trail through most of the canyon that makes for easy walking. This mostly limestone canyon is home to old growth ponderosa pine, with firs and occasional aspens clinging to the northern exposures.

From the tank on Kelly Canyon Road, start your journey into Kelly Canyon by walking downstream. The noise of the freeway will quickly dissipate as the canyon begins to form. Oak trees bend out from the base of rocky bluffs, and early in the season, a trickle of water can be heard underfoot. This canyon grows in depth and width as you continue along the gentle downhill grade. The game trail, which has as much human use as animal use, often provides easier walking than the creekbed. It is located on the sunnier side of the canyon, the right side. The creekbed is mostly small cobbles or gravel, so most of the water here is underground. There are no narrows in Kelly Canyon, but the occasional rock face and old growth forest provide a tranquil setting, making a visit here worthwhile.

At the confluence of Pumphouse Wash, turn right and head upstream to road #237 and your shuttle vehicle. If you didn't run a shuttle, turn around and enjoy Kelly Canyon from the opposite direction on the way back to the tank where you started.

*See map on page 89

Serenity

JAMES CANYON

General Description: A forested and rugged canyon near Flagstaff
Best Season: June—August, When it is hot, hot, hot!
Elevation: 6,600'—5,689'
Length: 7 miles. It is 4.5 miles down James, then another 2.6 miles down Pumphouse Wash to highway 89A.
Time Needed: 4—8 hours
Difficulty: Difficult—Technical (swimming, boulder hopping, scrambling, rappelling)
Shuttle: Optional
Maps: USGS: Mountainaire 7.5, USFS: Coconino N.F.

Access: Lower end: Drive south from Flagstaff on highway 89A about 14 miles to the bottom of the Oak Creek Canyon switchbacks. Park near the bridge over Pumphouse Wash.
 Upper end: Take I-17 south from Flagstaff about 9 miles. Exit onto Kelly Canyon Road, exit 331. Park here, near the freeway.

Trip Description: James Canyon is one of the headwater canyons of famous Oak Creek Canyon. It is a beautiful place of Coconino sandstone, draped in a pine/fir forest. This is an excellent canyon for first-time technical canyoneers. Though there are some big falls to rappel, there are also plenty of escape routes, so the canyon is less than fully committing.
 From Kelly Canyon road near exit 331, walk south, paralleling the freeway. In about 0.5 miles, you will be skidding down the slope into James Canyon. There are some pools in basalt here at the head of the canyon. Immediately downstream, the canyon's geology changes to Coconino sandstone. With the sandstone, the first fall appears. This obstacle is easily avoided on the right, but this sloping 10-foot fall into a pool might be a good place to hone your canyoneering skills. It requires a downclimb into a pool.
 The scenery is nice and the terrain is simple for the next 0.4 miles down to the first major fall of the canyon. It is a double drop; 12 feet into a slot, then another 7 feet into a pool. Rappel the first part of this drop, but consider downclimbing the 7-footer. It is easier to downclimb than to deal with rope while treading water. Not far below this pool, you'll enter some narrows with varying amounts of water in them. Depending on water level, it will be wading or swimming through most of these narrows. Plan on some scrambling between pools, too. The narrows finish with an 8-foot fall into a big pool.
 Travel eases for the next 0.5 miles, until the creekbed plummets in a sheer 40-foot falls. A good anchor for this rappel is the big fir tree on creek left. If things aren't going well at this point in the trip, there is an escape route to the rim on creek right.
 Below the 40-footer, the major difficulties are behind you, but the beauty is still present for the next 1.5 miles down to Pumphouse Wash.

Narrows start just around the corner. Expect to do at least some wading and possibly some swimming in here.

At the confluence of Pumphouse Wash, begin the boulder hop downstream. It is 2.6 miles to highway 89A. Though not as dramatic as James Canyon, Pumphouse is certainly worthy of exploration. Sculpted sandstone slabs and colorful walls accompany you all the way to the highway.

*See map on page 89

Rappelling the 40-footer in James Canyon

FRY CANYON

General Description: A quiet little canyon in the high country near
    Flagstaff
Best Season: May—November
Elevation: 7,000'—6,500'
Length: 3—4 miles round trip
Time Needed: 1—4 hours
Difficulty: Easy—Moderate (boulder hopping)
Shuttle: No
Maps: USGS: Mountainaire 7.5, Dutton Hill 7.5, USFS: Coconino N.F.

Access: Drive south from Flagstaff on highway 89A about 10 miles.
Between mileposts 392 and 393, Fry Canyon passes under the highway.
This is 0.3 miles north of milepost 392. Park off the highway on the south
side of the canyon.

Trip Description: Fry Canyon is primarily a pleasant walk in the woods. It
is a part of the Oak Creek drainage, which runs through Sedona and to the
Verde River.

There is a closed dirt road that runs along the south side of the canyon
for about 0.2 miles. After this, progress is best made up the creekbed.
Scrambling around deadfall is often necessary, and progress can be slow.

Maples are abundant in this canyon. In October they shed their leaves,
covering the forest floor with a blanket of red. Occasionally, an outcrop-
ping of limestone or sandstone will appear, only to quickly slip away into
the forest. This is a nice place to get a feeling of canyon solitude a short
distance from the highway.

FRY CANYON

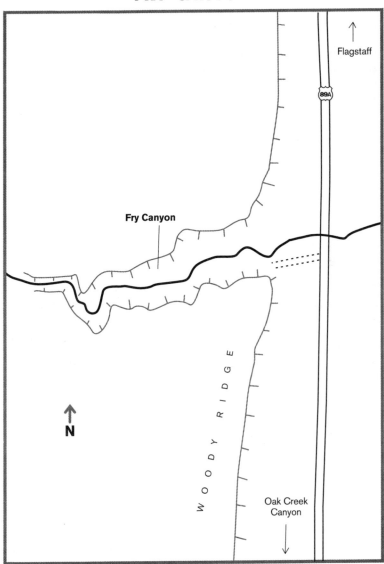

Fry Canyon

Flagstaff

89A

W O O D Y   R I D G E

N

Oak Creek
Canyon

main canyon bottom
side canyon bottom
trail
route
paved road
dirt road

tank spring guage

1 mile

STERLING CANYON

General Description: A steep, rarely visited canyon in upper Oak Creek Canyon

Best Season: April—November

Elevation: 7,100'—5,700'

Length: 3 miles to Sterling Springs one way

Time Needed: 2—4 hours one way 3.5—7 hours round trip

Difficulty: Moderate (climbing, boulder hopping)

Shuttle: Optional

Maps: USGS: Dutton Hill 7.5, Mountainaire 7.5, USFS: Coconino N.F.

Access: Take highway 89A south out of Flagstaff 10.5 miles to road #535. Turn right and follow #535 for 4.9 miles to road #535A and turn left. Take #535A 0.2 miles and turn left again, this time onto a rough dirt road that crosses some often-muddy low spots. Take this road 0.8 miles to Sterling Tank and park.

Lower end: Take 89A south from Flagstaff to the bottom of the switchbacks at the head of Oak Creek Canyon and park.

Trip Description: Walking downstream from Sterling Tank, you won't be in much of a canyon for the first couple of miles. It's just a creekbed in the forest with some mature ponderosa pines.

At about 1.7 miles, the creekbed plummets with a falls. This is where the canyon really begins. There is a scrambler's route just to the left of the main falls. From here down to Sterling Springs, the canyon drops 800 feet in 1.2 miles. To descend, you'll be scrambling down giant boulders most of the way. There are some big white firs, along with Douglas fir, aspen, and bigtooth maple in the cool canyon bottom. At the mouth of the canyon is Sterling Springs, the permanent water source for Oak Creek and home to a fish hatchery.

STERLING CANYON

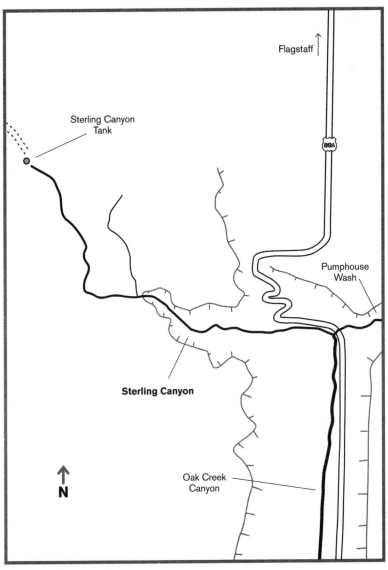

Flagstaff

Sterling Canyon
Tank

Pumphouse
Wash

Sterling Canyon

Oak Creek
Canyon

N

main canyon bottom	
side canyon bottom	
trail	
route	
paved road	
dirt road	

tank spring guage

1 mile

WEST FORK OF OAK CREEK

General Description: A deep canyon with huge sandstone walls, a running stream, and lush vegetation
Best Season: April—November (June—August: 80 degrees or hotter for the upper 1/3 of the canyon)
Elevation: 6,600'—5,200'
Length: 12 miles end to end
Time Needed: 7.5—11.5 hours or 2 days for end to end
Difficulty: Difficult in upper end (swimming) Easy in lower end
Shuttle: Yes (for end to end)
Maps: USGS: Dutton Hill 7.5, Wilson Mtn. 7.5, USFS: Coconino N.F.

Access: For the lower end, take highway 89A north out of Sedona, or south out of Flagstaff through Oak Creek Canyon. There is a parking lot for the West Fork (along with a $3.00 charge) on the west side of the highway 1.1 miles south of Cave Spring Campground, or 0.9 miles north of Don Hoel's Cabins.

For the upper end, take Woody Mtn. Rd. #231 south off old route 66 in west Flagstaff for 18.1 miles, where the road crosses the West Fork.

Trip Description: The West Fork is one of the most beautiful spots in Arizona. The wavelike sculpted banks of Supai sandstone along the creek have appeared in numerous hiking magazines and advertisements. The West Fork offers the best of both worlds, from hardwood forests of maple and oak in the canyon bottom, to hillsides of agave and cactus, all beneath towering formations of sandstone.

From the parking area in the lower end, a trail leads across Oak Creek and past the long ago burned Mayhew Lodge, then on up the canyon. The lower end of this canyon is very popular. Try to stay on the main trail to prevent erosion. The creek usually has just a small amount of water in it, but always enough to form gorgeous reflective pools. There is a huge diversity of plants here. Manzanita, prickly-pear cactus and Parry agave live on the south facing slopes, while Douglas fir, white fir, and ponderosa pine grow on northern exposures. Closer to the creek you'll find canyon maple, Gambel oak, and boxelder. The forest floor is covered in ferns and even *Cimicifuga arizonica*, the endangered and rare Arizona Bugbane.

The trail begins to fade as the canyon gets more rugged at about 4 miles. If your feet aren't wet already, they will be soon if you decide to continue upstream. Slippery boulders in the creekbed are eventually the only thing to walk on and pools begin to fill the canyon bottom. If you attempt the entire West Fork from end to end, you will encounter 5 deep pools. Two of these have routes around them, two must be swum, and one is usually about 5 feet deep—a chest deep wade for most people. These pools are always really cold—water temperature has been in the 40s or low 50s whenever I've been there.

The upper 2 miles of the West Fork is a beautiful forest walk, with Englemann spruce—a tree normally found above 9,000 feet, on the northern exposures, and old growth ponderosa pine on the southern exposures.

Campsites are limited in the upper half of the canyon and camping is not allowed in the lower 6 miles. Water is intermittent in the upper half of the canyon.

A chest deep wade in the upper West Fork

West Fork of Oak Creek

WEST FORK

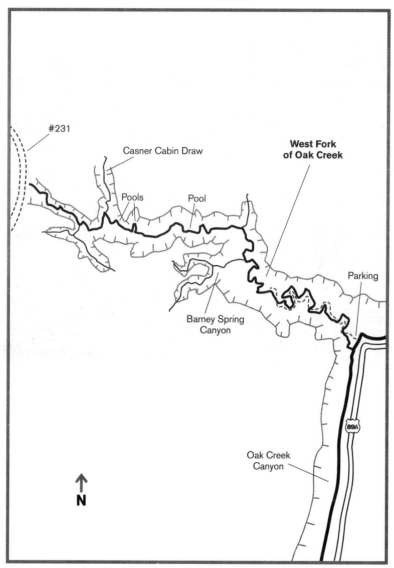

#231

Casner Cabin Draw

**West Fork
of Oak Creek**

Pools

Pool

Parking

Barney Spring
Canyon

89A

Oak Creek
Canyon

↑
N

main canyon bottom
side canyon bottom
trail
route
paved road
dirt road

●   ♂   ⊗
tank spring guage

1 mile

LOY CANYON

General Description: A trail hike with views of redrocks and the upper Verde Valley
Best Season: October—April
Elevation: 6,400'—4,700'
Length: 9 miles round trip to Secret Saddle
Time Needed: 3.5—7 hours
Difficulty: Easy
Shuttle: No
Maps: USGS: Loy Butte 7.5, USFS: Coconino N.F.

Access: From Sedona, drive toward Cottonwood about 10 miles on highway 89A. Take forest road #525 north for about 10 miles to the trailhead at the edge of Hancock ranch.

Trip Description: Trail #5 leads through junipers in the mostly flat canyon bottom. There are some impressive views to the east of the cliffs that guard Secret Mountain. At about 3 miles, the trail begins to climb. At 3.5 miles, it switchbacks up the slope to the north of the creekbed. Because this slope is direct southern exposure, you can hike here throughout the winter in most years. At the head of Loy Canyon, you'll reach Secret Saddle, the turnaround point. If you're prepared for more exploration, the upper reaches of Secret Canyon lie to the northeast. Secret Mountain is to the south.

Since this canyon is further from Sedona than most of the other redrock canyons, it is less crowded. Keep your eyes peeled for javelina browsing the canyon bottom. There are also many ruins on Loy Butte, to the west.

LOY CANYON

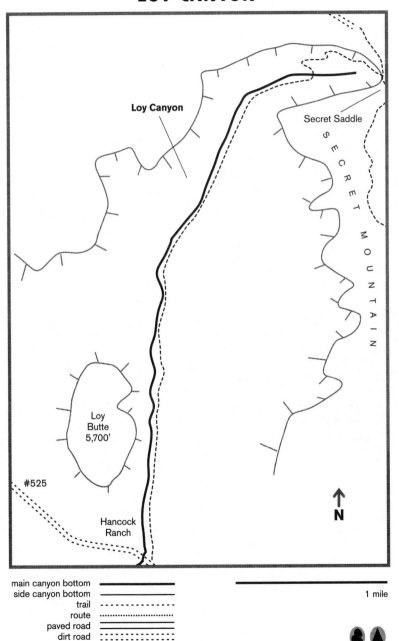

Loy Canyon

Secret Saddle

S E C R E T   M O U N T A I N

Loy
Butte
5,700'

#525

Hancock
Ranch

N

main canyon bottom
side canyon bottom
trail
route
paved road
dirt road

1 mile

tank   spring   guage

SECRET CANYON

General Description: A point to point backpack through a deep, forested sandstone canyon
Best Season: April—October
Elevation: 6,600'—4,700'
Length: 10 miles
Time Needed: 2 days
Difficulty: Moderate—Difficult (route finding, boulder hopping)
Shuttle: Yes
Maps: USGS: Loy Butte 7.5, Wilson Mountain 7.5, USFS: Coconino N.F.

Access: Lower end: Take Dry Creek Road off highway 89A in Sedona. At 2 miles from 89A, take road #152 for 3.4 miles to the Secret Canyon trailhead. This is where you can finish a Secret Canyon trip. Or, if you only have a day, this is a good place to explore the lower end of Secret.

Upper end: Take Woody Mountain Road #231 south from route 66 out of Flagstaff for 20.2 miles. Go right on #231A, and using roads #231A and #538D, proceed 3.2 miles to road #538. Head left, or south on #538 and follow it to its end in 5.2 miles. Park here, at the trailhead for Secret Mountain and Loy Canyon.

Trip Description: Secret Canyon is tucked in the middle of the Red Rock Secret Mountain Wilderness. It is quite similar in many ways to the famous and spectacular West Fork of Oak Creek to the north. Both have big sandstone walls, dense canyon bottom vegetation, and unique erosional formations in the Supai sandstone. Of the two, however, the West Fork is blessed with perennial water in the creek. Secret is also harder to get into, with a very steep descent required in the upper end, and a dusty 2-mile march through chaparral at the lower end.

From the parking spot in the upper end, drop straight in to Secret Canyon, which is just east of road #538. This descent is one of the more difficult parts of the route. Though there are no cliffbands to work around, the slope is consistently steep and the soil is likely to give way, so go slowly and be careful with your footing.

Less than a quarter mile downstream from the route in, there are some narrows and a fall of about 12 feet in the Coconino sandstone. A log should be wedged against this fall to assist in your downclimb. This log can serve as a reminder of what can happen in this rugged terrain.

A solo canyoneer—Ken Webb—was making his descent into Secret Canyon via a gully on the north side when the rain soaked slope he was on slid away beneath him. He grasped desperately at the trees lining the gully, but gravity and the weight of his pack conspired to keep him sliding and falling at ever increasing speeds toward the canyon bottom. The only sounds echoing through this lonely canyon were those of rocks tumbling and the air being punched out of Ken's lungs with every impact. Suddenly, the plummeting stopped, and he covered his head, bracing for the avalanche of rocks he was sure was going to end these last few harrowing moments of his life.

But the crush never came. Miraculously, he had survived a fall of 50 feet by landing on his pack out of the slide path of the gully. Still pumped from the adrenaline in his bloodstream, he got up and started walking almost immediately. It took a minute or two to notice the burning pressure in his ankle and the numerous scrapes from head to toe. He was making progress hobbling upstream until faced with a sandstone drop-off. It was a mere 12 feet high, but nearly vertical. The thought of another fall while attempting to climb this rock with only one good leg was nauseating. Yet what other option was there?

He began to look around for another way out when he saw, leaning against the slope, a log about 14 feet long, perfectly manageable, yet sturdy enough to climb on. Wedging it solidly against the falls, he crawled his way up the newly formed ramp and eventually out of Secret Canyon.

Ken's log should still be there to assist in your downclimb. If it is gone, the climb will be much more difficult, but still negotiable—a fifth class downclimb.

There is usually not much water in the creekbed until the red Supai sandstone appears. In the Supai, there will be occasional pools, some of which may require a detour to get around. I walked across logs to keep dry on 2 pools, and scrambled around a couple more. There are several sets of enchanting little narrows in the Supai, as well as side canyons worthy of exploration.

Campsites get more plentiful towards the lower end, and a trail develops about 2 or 3 miles from the mouth. This will lead into the open red rock country, and then on to Dry Creek Road.

The only distraction to this magical place are the tourist helicopters out of Sedona. These menaces of the air fly up Secret Canyon at an obnoxiously low altitude, destroying the wilderness feel in an otherwise tranquil setting. One can only hope their business is bad on the day you choose to visit Secret Canyon.

SECRET CANYON

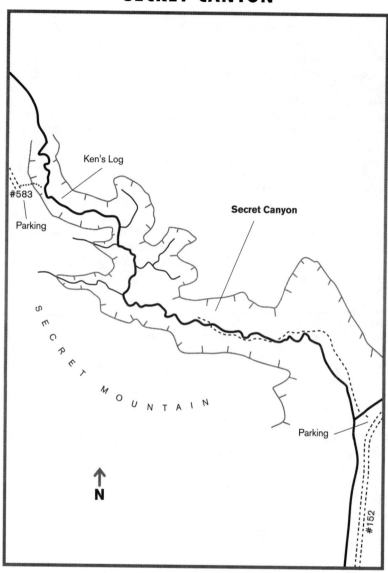

Ken's Log

#583

Parking

Secret Canyon

S E C R E T   M O U N T A I N

Parking

↑
N

#152

1 mile

main canyon bottom
side canyon bottom
trail
route
paved road
dirt road

tank spring guage

Secret Canyon narrows

BOYNTON CANYON

General Description: A spectacular and popular day hike near Sedona
Best Season: All year
Elevation: 5,200'—4,600'
Time Needed: 1.5—5 hours
Length: 5 miles round trip
Difficulty: Easy
Shuttle: No
Maps: USGS: Wilson Mtn. 7.5, Loy Butte 7.5, USFS: Coconino N.F.

Access: Take Dry Creek Road north—northwest off highway 89A in
Sedona. At 2.9 miles from 89A, go left at the first T intersection. In another 1.6 miles at the second T, go right. There is a parking area and trailhead in another 0.3 miles on the right.

Trip Description: Boynton Canyon is one of the neatest hikes in the
Sedona area. Unfortunately, everyone seems to know this. It's not the place
to go if you want to avoid humans. However, if you are looking for a
pleasant canyon hike in some awesome scenery directly off the pavement,
as a famous pioneer to our north once said, "This is the place."
    The trail begins by winding through the chaparral, staying to the west
of a tennis resort. Once this private property is passed, the trail stays on
the canyon floor the rest of the way. The scenery gets more dramatic the
further you go, until at last the trail peters out and the canyon ends
abruptly, surrounded by the 800-foot cliffs guarding Bear Mountain. The
sun filters down past the cliffs, through the tops of the Douglas fir, and
illuminates a forest floor of pine needles at the foot of a 400 year old ponderosa. Even if you must share this spot with your neighbor, it's worth it.

Red rock vistas surround Boynton Canyon.

BOYNTON CANYON

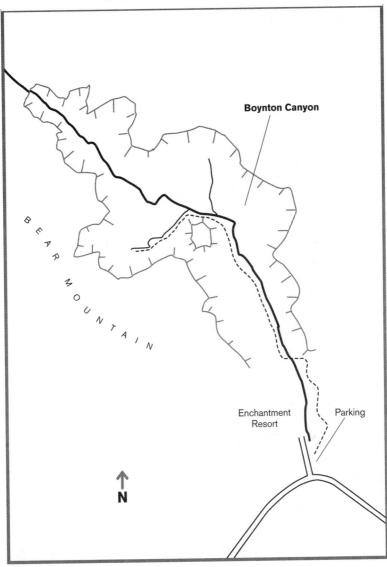

Boynton Canyon

BEAR MOUNTAIN

Enchantment Resort

Parking

N

main canyon bottom
side canyon bottom
trail
route
paved road
dirt road

tank spring guage

1 mile

MUNDS CANYON

General Description: A little-visited, varied canyon 18 miles from Flagstaff
Best Season: May—mid November
Elevation: 6,500'—4,900'
Length: 8 miles round trip
Time Needed: 3.5—7 hours round trip
Difficulty: Moderate (boulder hopping, scrambling)
Shuttle: No
Maps: USGS: Munds Park 7.5, USFS: Coconino N.F.

Access: Take I-17 south from Flagstaff about 17 miles to Munds Park. Park off the freeway near the bridge that spans Munds Canyon.

Trip Description: Munds Canyon has several faces. Up high, the canyon is a basalt gorge filled with maples and pools of water. As you descend through the Coconino sandstone, there are some narrow spots and a couple of small falls. Lower yet, sycamores cling to the sides of the creekbed and views of Wilson Mountain and the red Supai sandstone dominate.

For the entire length of Munds Canyon, you will be hopping between big gray boulders that jam the creekbed. A couple miles down from the freeway, there are some narrows in the basalt that hold permanent pools. You'll have to be creative if you want to keep your feet dry bypassing these pools. Shortly after power lines cross high above the canyon, the Coconino sandstone appears. There are some short narrows in this section and falls that are easily negotiated. There is a route leading down a gully on creek left at the falls. When you see the red Supai sandstone at creek level, start thinking about turning around. There is private property about 1.5 miles downstream.

Return the way you came, back up the creek, or find a route out and walk back on top of the plateau. There is a route out of the canyon 0.3 miles upstream of the powerlines, on the north side.

Munds Canyon empties into Oak Creek just upstream from the Indian Gardens historical marker, but access is blocked at this end by private property.

MUNDS

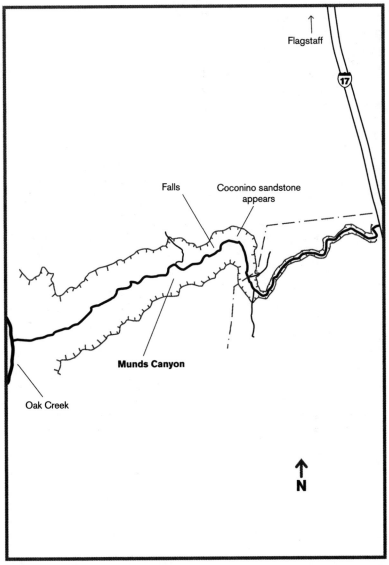

Flagstaff

17

Falls

Coconino sandstone
appears

Munds Canyon

Oak Creek

N

main canyon bottom
side canyon bottom
trail
route
paved road
dirt road

tank spring guage

1 mile

WOODS CANYON

General Description: A formidable canyon with pools, ruins, and isolation
Best Season: mid May—September
Elevation: 6,400'—4,000'
Length: 15 miles from I-17 to the trail #93 trailhead
Time Needed: 2 days or 1 long day to traverse the entire canyon (9—11 hours if you're in good shape)
Difficulty: Difficult (swimming, scrambling, boulder hopping)
Shuttle: Optional
Maps: USGS: Munds Mtn. 7.5 (Sedona 7.5)., USFS: Coconino N.F.

Access: Upper end: Take I-17 south from Flagstaff about 24 miles, exit on Rocky Park Road, exit 315. Take road #80, which heads north paralleling the freeway. Take this rocky road for about 1.7 miles and park.

Lower end: From Flagstaff, head south on I-17 about 40 miles to exit 298. Head northwest towards Sedona on route 179. In 3.6 miles, highway 179 crosses Dry Beaver Creek, which is the creekbed of Woods Canyon. In 2.3 more miles, there is a wide spot with a gate and dirt road heading east towards the creek. Turn here. This road is about 1.0—1.5 miles from the Village of Oak Creek. Proceed through the gate, and follow the dirt road to its end in 1.2 miles. Trail #93 starts here.

Trip Description: Woods Canyon runs northeast to southwest between I-17 and Sedona. Despite its proximity to these well—travelled areas, it remains wild, concealed beneath plateaus of juniper and pine. Between its walls are deep pools, undisturbed ruins, and wild-eyed animals. I once encountered deer, elk, eagles, and bears in Woods Canyon all in the same day!

Once you enter the bowels of this gorge, there are no easy ways out. Probably the best way to explore this canyon is end-to-end, entering near I-17 and going downstream all the way to highway 179, with trail #93 leading you out the last 5 miles. The only problem with this option is that the lower end would be brutally hot in the summer, which is the only time of year a Woods Canyon traverse is feasible, due to pools upstream. You could make an out and back trip into Woods from the upper end, but swimming the pool in the Coconino sandstone is bad enough once, the thought of swimming it twice turns my stomach. I have used the steep gullies that lead to the rim just below the Supai pools as exit routes, but they are arduous ascents through chaparral. I wouldn't recommend them. We once tried to enter Woods Canyon from the west, coming over Horse Mesa and making a bushwhacking descent to the canyon floor. The temperatures were in the upper 90s, and by the time we made it to the Supai pools, our tongues were swelling from dehydration in the intense heat. Our hike back turned into a true death march. A near miss with a rattlesnake put our nerves on edge as we crashed through the chaparral back to Horse

Mesa. We finally made a risky decision to explore an unknown route off the mesa in the fading twilight. The gamble paid off, and we made it to the car as darkness fell. It took two days to rehydrate from the ordeal. End-to-end seems like the best option.

From road #80, walk to the northwest through the pines, and you will hit the rim of Woods Canyon in about 0.5 miles. You may have to work around some cliffs of basalt, but some basic route finding and scrambling will quickly have you in the canyon bottom.

You will find pools in the basalt in the first 3 miles of Woods. Most of the time, these pools can all be scrambled around. If you are there soon after the creek has run, some wading may be necessary. This part of the canyon requires almost constant boulder hopping in the jumbled gray basalt of the riverbed.

About a quarter of a mile below where a big side canyon from the south enters, there is a 70-foot sloping fall in the basalt. Either rappel this fall, or scramble across the slope on creek left. This slope is steep, but by watching your step carefully and using the trees as handholds, you can make a traverse.

Shortly below the falls, the Coconino sandstone arrives, and along with it, some short narrows. This first set of narrows is dry, the next set 0.5 miles downstream is not. A deep pool of frigid water spans from wall to wall. I highly recommend a drysuit or at least a wetsuit for swimming this pool. It is long and very cold—colder than any other pool in this book. If you haven't been turned back by the pool of liquid ice, another waits downstream. However, this second pool is much shallower, and will only be knee-deep unless you are on the heels of runoff.

Soon the canyon cuts below the Coconino sandstone and into the Supai. The Supai sandstone houses some wonderful narrows and shallow pools. None of these pools are mandatory swims—there are routes around them all—but on a hot day, they are extremely inviting swims.

Look for a Sinaguan Indian ruin about 150 yards below the last Supai pool, on the right. These ancient Arizonans inhabited dwellings such as this until the year 1200, when most moved to larger communities such as Tuzigoot or Montezuma Castle in the Verde Valley.

It is about 4 more miles of boulder hopping down the dry creekbed before trail #93 begins to form. This trail leads 5 more miles to highway 179.

WOODS CANYON

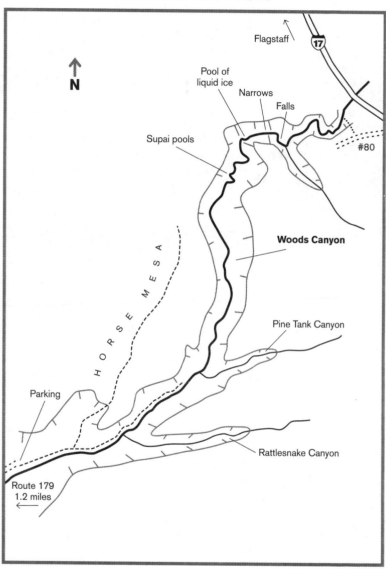

N

Flagstaff

17

Pool of
liquid ice

Narrows

Falls

Supai pools

#80

Woods Canyon

H O R S E   M E S A

Pine Tank Canyon

Parking

Rattlesnake Canyon

Route 179
1.2 miles

1 mile

main canyon bottom	▬▬▬
side canyon bottom	───
trail	- - - - -
route	··········
paved road	═══
dirt road	▪▪▪▪▪

● tank   ⚲ spring   ⊗ guage

Woods Canyon hides beneath wooded plateaus.

WET BEAVER CREEK

General Description: A wild canyon featuring riparian growth and clear deep pools
Best Season: June—September
Elevation: 6,100'—3,900' (creek elevation 5,000'—3,900')
Length: 15 miles one way, 24 miles for loop
Time Needed: 2 days (8.5—13 hours for the strong hiker's mega—day) 3 days for loop route
Difficulty: Difficult (climbing, swimming, extensive boulder hopping)
Shuttle: Yes (no for loop)
Maps: USGS: Casner Butte 7.5, Apache Maid Mtn. 7.5, USFS: Coconino N.F.

Access: Lower end: Take exit #298 off I-17 and drive east toward Wet Beaver Creek. In 2 miles, turn left following signs for the Bell trailhead. The parking area is 0.3 miles further. Don't leave valuables at the Bell trailhead. Thieves frequent the area.

Upper end: Take the Stoneman Lake exit #306 off I-17 and drive east on this paved road for 6.4 miles. The road turns to dirt here. Go right on road #229 and stay right on #229 at the junction in 4.6 miles. In another 0.4 miles, turn right onto road #620. Follow road #620 for 1.6 miles and make a left onto a secondary dirt road just before the climb up Apache Maid Mountain. Take this bouldery road for 0.5 miles to the bottom of the grassy hill and bear left, then straight for another 0.8 miles toward the broad valley ahead. Two wheel drives will likely want to stop at the rocky gulch with ponderosa pines. Four wheel drives could continue about another 0.7 miles to the top of Waldroup Canyon.

Trip Description: Wet Beaver Creek is a refreshing watery route slicing through the Mogollon Rim. There are two approaches to a Wet Beaver Creek hike: loop or point to point. I've done both and prefer running a shuttle and going point to point. However, the loop route has its advantages; saving gas, money, and vehicle abuse. It also gives a greater appreciation of the creek after spending a day of walking through dry juniper hill country.

To do the loop, start at the Bell trail and head upstream a couple miles to the Apache Maid trail. Take the Apache Maid up out of the canyon. Here, it tends to fade into old ranch roads. Some route finding is needed to make your way northeast, then east over a pass to the north of Hog Hill. From here, you'll drop into Waldroup Valley at the head of Waldroup Canyon.

If you've driven into the upper end and parked at the rocky gulch with ponderosas, walk down the road passing Mullican Tank, a burned-out cabin and Waldroup Place Tank en route to the head of Waldroup Canyon. The head of Waldroup Canyon is about 0.7 miles from the rocky ponderosa gulch.

Heading down Waldroup Canyon, vast basalt amphitheaters loom overhead. Shady copses of Arizona walnut and Gambel oak adorn the edges of the creekbed, and carpets of grapevine blanket the boulders underfoot. There are 7 falls to negotiate in Waldroup Canyon. All of them are in the basalt, except the last, which is in limestone. Every fall except one is either a 4th class scramble, or it has a route around. The fifth fall is the exception. Here, a heinous chaparral-choked route on the left is the only option other than the 5.0 downclimb at the falls.

At the bottom of Waldroup Canyon, Wet Beaver Creek is a dry boulder field with a few scattered sycamores. In less than a mile downstream, water springs up and a cold clear pool chills you up to your waist. Don't be discouraged by the cold water, it gets progressively warmer as you proceed downstream.

There are over a dozen deep pools and countless more to wade through between here and Bell Crossing—9 miles distant. The water is a refreshing yet comfortable temperature, much warmer than Wet Beaver's big brother to the south—West Clear Creek. In descending Wet Beaver Creek, a canyoneer will find that idyllic moments of lolling by monkey flower-lined cascades are broken by long stretches of aggressive boulder hopping and hacking through willows. Most of the pools are in Coconino sandstone, but some of the most memorable are found in the Supai sandstone. Campsites are limited and small throughout the canyon.

Bell Crossing is easy to recognize. It is the final deep and lovely Supai pool, and it has a route to the right of it. There are usually people here, too, and along with them, trash. Please help out the slobs and pack out any garbage you might see. From Bell Crossing, it is another 4 miles down the Bell trail to the parking area.

WET BEAVER CREEK

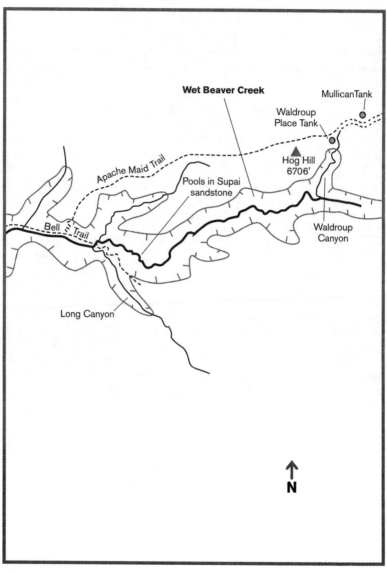

MullicanTank

Wet Beaver Creek

Waldroup
Place Tank

Apache Maid Trail

Hog Hill
6706'

Pools in Supai
sandstone

Waldroup
Canyon

Bell Trail

Long Canyon

N

1 mile

main canyon bottom	
side canyon bottom	
trail	- - - - - - - -
route	....
paved road	
dirt road	

● ⚲ ⊗
tank spring guage

Swimming through Wet Beaver Creek

WILLOW VALLEY

General Description: A narrow and thickly forested canyon on the head-waters of West Clear Creek

Best Season: June—early July (hot, but no thunderstorms)

Elevation: 6,760'—6,000'

Length: 6.5 miles

Time Needed: 4—8 hours

Difficulty: Difficult (scrambling, swimming)

Shuttle: Optional. The shuttle distance is about 3 miles on dirt roads. This is an excellent choice for a bike shuttle. You could also walk it.

Maps: USGS: Calloway Butte 7.5, USFS: Coconino N.F.

Access: Take Lake Mary Road south from Flagstaff. About seven miles south of Happy Jack, turn left on forest road #81. This turn is about 10 miles north of Clint's Well, and just north of a bridge over upper Willow Valley Creek. Take road #81 for 3.1 miles and veer left on road #81E. Continue on #81E for 3.8 miles to the junction of road #693. Stay left, in another 0.5 miles you will be at the junction of the Maxwell Trail Road and the Maxwell Tank Road. If you want to leave a shuttle vehicle at the Maxwell trailhead, take the road to the right and proceed about 1.5 miles to the canyon rim. For the start of the hike, go left towards Maxwell Tank. At 0.9 miles, bear left, Maxwell Tank is 0.4 miles further.

Trip Description: This trip takes you through possibly the narrowest valley in the world. Whoever named this a valley obviously had never travelled through the depths of this high country gorge. Cliffs of Coconino sand-stone pinch together in moss covered depths, and pools stretch from wall to wall in places.

From Maxwell Tank, make your way downstream, toward Willow Valley. Pick your route carefully in Maxwell Tank Canyon to avoid the sticker bush-es, technically *Robinia neomexicana*, or New Mexico Locust. It is prolific in this side canyon since a forest fire came through several years ago.

Just above the confluence with Willow Valley, there is a small cliff (10 ft.) of limestone to work through. If you are a climber, you'll want to downclimb. Otherwise, make your way down a gully on the left and do battle with the locust.

Once in the bottom of Willow Valley, the cliffs of Coconino sandstone will begin to close in. Less than 0.5 miles from Maxwell Tank Canyon you'll arrive at the first of 4 major pools. There are climbing routes (5.0—5.2) to the right of the first 2 pools, but the third pool is a mandatory swim. The fourth pool has no climbing routes either, but it is only a few feet deep, demanding a wade. All four of these pools lie within a 0.2 mile stretch of Coconino narrows which is the most dramatic scenery of the trip.

Below the last pool the canyon meanders for about 1.5 miles, and run-ning water surfaces just before hitting "the straight-away." This is an easily recognizable section of canyon where the rims open up and things almost do resemble a valley. Slopes of white fir tumble down to the creekbed and campsites appear, tucked away in the dark greenery. A trail begins to form below the straight-away, and walking gets easier down to the confluence of Clover Creek. It is here where Willow Valley and Clover creeks merge to form West Clear Creek.

Another 0.5 miles of pleasant boulder hopping along the banks of Clear Creek brings you to the Maxwell trail. Look for a trail leading up through the ponderosas on river right a couple hundred yards before the canyon makes a left hand turn. The Maxwell trail is a 0.6 mile climb to the rim of the canyon and your shuttle vehicle, if you left one. Otherwise, it is 2.5—3.0 miles of road walking back to Maxwell Tank.

WILLOW VALLEY

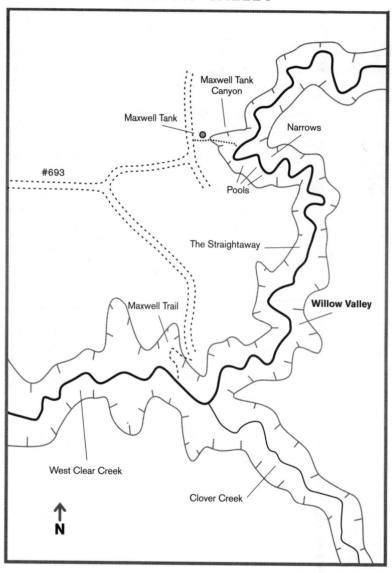

Maxwell Tank
Canyon

Maxwell Tank

Narrows

#693

Pools

The Straightaway

Maxwell Trail

Willow Valley

West Clear Creek

Clover Creek

N

1 mile

main canyon bottom	
side canyon bottom	
trail	
route	
paved road	
dirt road	

tank   spring   guage

Lisa Gelczis

A canyoneer is dwarfed by the walls in Willow Valley.

WEST CLEAR CREEK

overview

West Clear Creek is the classic Mogollon Rim canyon. Coconino sandstone narrows, cold clear pools, lush canyon bottom vegetation, and pure cliffside springs—West Clear Creek has it all.

From forests of fir in the upper reaches to open desert grasslands in the lower end, several vegetative communities are found here. The canyon is primarily in Coconino sandstone, with Supai sandstone appearing in the lower central portion. Prominent cliffs of basalt form formidable rims in the central and lower sections. Water is a striking feature along the length of this canyon, in places forming wall-to-wall pools hundreds of feet long. To traverse the entire canyon, from Clear Creek's origin to Bull Pen Ranch at the lower end, would be about 30 miles, or 3 to 6 days of travel.

As with Sycamore Canyon, I have divided this canyon into 4 sections as follows:

Headwaters: Willow Valley and Clover Creeks - Trail at road #142E
Upper West Clear Creek: Road #142E - Trail #33
Central West Clear Creek: Trail #33 - Trail #17
Lower West Clear Creek: Trail #17 - Bull Pen Ranch

Hesitating before taking the plunge

WEST CLEAR CREEK

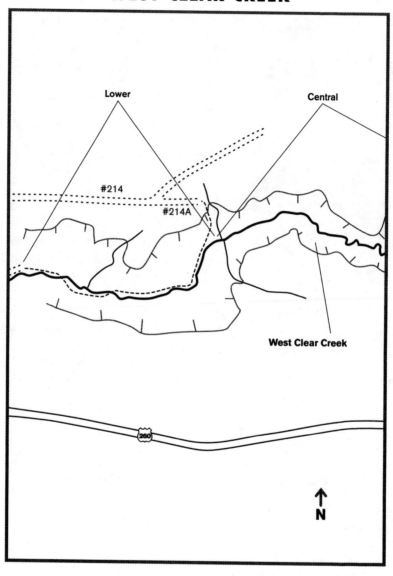

Lower

Central

#214

#214A

West Clear Creek

260

N

main canyon bottom	
side canyon bottom	
trail	
route	
paved road	
dirt road	

tank spring guage

WEST CLEAR CREEK

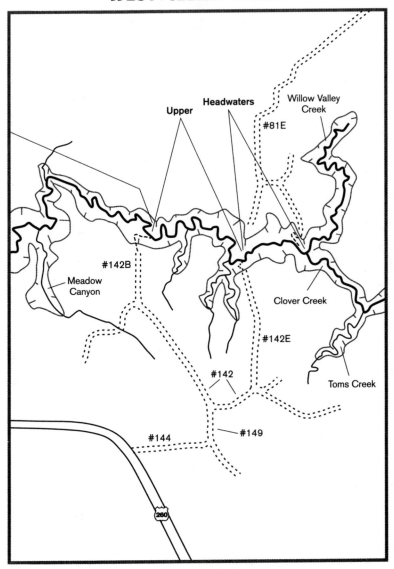

Upper

Headwaters

Willow Valley
Creek

#81E

#142B

Meadow
Canyon

Clover Creek

#142E

#142

Toms Creek

#144

#149

260

1 mile

WEST CLEAR CREEK
headwaters

General Description: A canyon with dense greenery and plenty of water
Best Season: mid—April through October
Elevation: 6,540'—5,900' (creek elevation 6,000'—5,900')
Length: 6.5 miles round trip (3 miles one way along creek)
Time Needed: 3—8 hours round trip
Difficulty: Moderate (wading, boulder hopping)
Shuttle: Optional. You could leave a vehicle at the Maxwell trail, (See Willow Valley description for directions) but that would be a very long shuttle for such a short hike
Maps: USGS: Calloway Butte 7.5, USFS: Coconino N.F.

Access: There are several ways to gain access to this section of canyon. The route described here brings you in at the downstream end of this segment, with a steep but short trail. Additional access points are via the Tramway trail #32 and the Maxwell trail #37, both on the north side of the canyon. You may also enter via one of West Clear Creek's tributaries, Willow Valley Creek or Clover Creek.

To get to the trailhead on road #142E, begin by taking highway 260 east from the 260 and 87 junction located north of Strawberry, AZ for 3.1 miles. Turn right on road #144. This is 0.1 miles west of milepost 249. Take road #144 1.8 miles to the junction of road #149. Turn left on road #149 and follow it 1.2 miles to road #142. Turn right at the Y intersection of road #142 and follow it 1 mile to road #142E. Make a left on #142E and follow it to the end in 2.7 miles.

Trip Description: This uppermost portion of West Clear Creek is home to lush shade-loving vegetation, clear pools of trout, and petroglyph panels. There is a footpath along the creek for most of this stretch, laid down by the many trout fisherman who frequent the area.

From the trailhead at the end of road #142E, it is a steep descent to the canyon bottom. This is the steepest trail into West Clear Creek, and if it is wet it can be treacherous. Notice the giant white firs on the way down.

At the creek, head upstream. There is a side canyon worth a visit in 0.3 miles, on creek left. A huge falls about 100 yards up this side canyon gushes with water during certain times of the year.

Back in the main canyon, the easiest route will often lead you across benchlands above the creek. These flat benches are home to a lush forest of Douglas fir, boxelder, canyon maple, and Gambel oak. Some of the greenery underfoot is bracken fern, false hellebore, and horsetail, which looks like little green straws growing out of the ground.

The canyon is generally mellow through here, lacking any tight narrows or deep pools. You will, however, be forced to wade across the creek a few times. The fisherman's trail fades in places, and you may find yourself bushwhacking through jungle-thick riparian vegetation occasionally.

There is a large panel of petroglyphs on creek right, just upstream from Tramway Canyon. Some nimwit built a campfire at the base of the petroglyph wall, obscuring some of them in soot, but many remain in fine condition.

Three miles up from your entry point, you'll arrive at the confluence of Clover and Willow Valley creeks. This spot may be hard to recognize if you haven't followed your map carefully. There is a long gravel bar on creek left, and at the upstream end of this gravel bar, a small stream comes in, also on creek left. This small stream is Clover Creek. The major canyon to your north is Willow Valley. You are now at the origin of West Clear Creek. From here you may return back downstream to the #142E trail, or explore further, up either Willow Valley or Clover Creek.

Dense forests surround West Clear Creek.

WEST CLEAR CREEK

upper

General Description: A well-watered canyon with varied scenery
Best Season: mid—May to mid—September
Elevation: 6,540'—5,700' (creek elevation 5,900' - 5,700')
Length: 6 miles one way, 12 miles round trip
Time Needed: 3.5—8 hours or 2 days, one way
Difficulty: Moderate—Difficult (wading, swimming, boulder hopping)
Shuttle: Optional. Access for the lower end of this section is via road
   #142B, which is a rocky 4-wheel-drive road. Therefore, two 4-wheel-
   drive vehicles would be necessary for a car shuttle. A bike shuttle could
   be an option—it would be 8 miles.
Maps: USGS: Calloway Butte 7.5, USFS: Coconino N.F.

Access: Upper access point: Take highway 260 northwest from the 260
and 87 junction for 3.1 miles. Turn east on road #144 and follow it 1.8
miles to road #149. Turn left on #149 and follow it 1.2 miles to road
#142. Turn right, or east, at #142 and follow it 1 mile to #142E. Take a
left on #142E and follow it to its end in 2.7 miles.
   Lower access point: From the junction of roads #149 and #142, (see
above directions) head west on #142 for 2.8 miles to road #142B. Follow
#142B north for about 2—2.5 miles to the canyon rim and trail #33. I
don't know the exact mileage down #142B to the canyon. I biked down
this road because it is very rocky and requires at least a high clearance
vehicle, if not 4-wheel-drive. I estimate the mileage from road #142 to trail
#33 to be 2.3 miles. There are a few ranch roads that branch off from
#142B, but #142B is usually signed well. Look for the signs carefully, and
you should be able to stay on #142B.

Trip Description: This section of West Clear Creek is a canyon in transition.
It is not as lush as the segment upstream, or as steep and rugged as the
segment downstream, but it has a little of both. This portion of the canyon
has a short section of narrows, many pools to wade or swim, and a very
open stretch. Good campsites are scattered, but there are some.
   From the terminus of road #142E, follow the steep trail to the canyon
bottom. This trail is the steepest of all that enter this canyon, and it can be
slick if it is wet. Be careful, and enjoy the giant white firs you'll pass on
your descent.
   At the creek, head downstream through the always invigorating pools
of Clear Creek. You'll be wading lots in this section, but swimming only
once. About 1.2 miles down, there is a wall to wall pool that requires a
short swim. It will be cold, but brief.
   Just below this pool is "the pillar," a rock spire incongruously sitting at
creek level. The creek then meanders for about a mile before going into a

short stretch of narrows. You'll most likely just have to wade some hip deep pools through these narrows. Remember, though, a riverbed changes with every flood, and I'm sure West Clear Creek has flooded since I've written this description, so finding a deep pool in here is not out of the question.

The canyon opens and makes a sharp turn to the southwest shortly below the narrows. You'll want to seek out the trail on river right through here to avoid the impenetrable riparian vegetation in the creek bottom. Once things begin to close in again, and you find yourself back in the creek, it is 1 more mile of wading and boulder hopping to trail #33. There are usually cairns placed to mark this trail on creek left. It exits just before the canyon makes a sharp right hand turn.

Return the way you came, or if you ran a shuttle, ascend trail #33. Or, if you are combining this part of the canyon with the central section, continue downstream—the best is yet to come.

Wading in West Clear Creek

WEST CLEAR CREEK
central

General Description: A wild and beautiful canyon with narrows, pools, and springs
Best Season: June—September. Watch for flash floods during monsoon season.
Elevation: 6,380'—4,100' (creek elevation 5,700' - 4,100')
Length: 16 creek miles. Trail #33 is about 0.5 miles. Trail #17 is about 2 miles from the creek to the road.
Time Needed: 2.5—4 days
Difficulty: Difficult (boulder hopping, swimming, scrambling)
Shuttle: Yes. This shuttle is a tad long, but not too bad considering that you'll be out a few days.
Maps: USGS: Calloway Butte 7.5, Buckhorn Mtn. 7.5, Walker Mtn. 7.5, USFS: Coconino N.F.

Access: Lower end: From Camp Verde, take highway 260 to the east about 5 miles and turn left on forest road #618. Take road #618 for 4.2 miles and make a right onto road #214. Follow #214 for 5.3 miles to #214A. Take road #214A about 1.3 miles to the trail #17 parking area. Road #214A is rocky, requiring high clearance vehicles.

Upper end: On highway 260, at a point 3.1 miles from the junction of highway 87 north of Strawberry, AZ, turn east onto forest road #144. Follow #144 for 1.8 miles to road #149. Turn left on #149 and follow it 1.2 miles to road #142. Turn left, or west on #142 and go 2.8 miles to road #142B. Follow #142B north for about 2.0—2.5 miles to the canyon rim and trail #33. I don't know the exact mileage down #142B to the canyon. I biked down this road because it is very rocky and requires at least a high clearance vehicle, if not 4-wheel-drive. I estimate the mileage from #142 to trail #33 to be 2.3 miles.

Trip Description: This is the heart of West Clear Creek. Sandstone sidewalks lead to pools that are both lengthy and cold. Springs shower into the canyon from lush grottoes, and the creek froths and splashes down slides of red Supai sandstone.

Trail #33 switchbacks down 680 vertical feet into a rugged section of canyon dominated by tan and orange-hued Coconino sandstone. Douglas firs crowd the steep slopes pouring into the canyon, and sheer cliffs of cross-bedded sandstone rise straight out of a pool. This scene repeats frequently over the next 3 miles. Wading is an almost constant task, and swimming often offers the best path of travel.

A few miles down from trail #33, there is a nice campsite where the powerlines cross the canyon. I only mention this because campsites are limited for the next 3 miles downstream.

The canyon mellows near the long straight-away about 1.5 miles below the powerlines. Basalt covers the sandstone cliffs, and the rim lowers, sitting only 200 feet above the creek. This gentle stretch of canyon is merely the calm before the storm, however. Just before the canyon makes a 90-degree turn to the south, things get really interesting. Canyon walls close in, and the narrow defile is filled with frigid clear water. The longest pool in all of West Clear Creek is in this section. Called "The White Box" due to the pale colored sandstone framing it, this water hole snakes its way between the canyon walls for 70 yards.

The creek continues to tumble through varied geology for the next several miles to trail #17. Coconino sandstone walkways relent to gray and black basalt boulders that pack the creekbed. Supai sandstone begins to peek out here and there, gradually becoming more prominent as you travel downstream, until an inner gorge of Supai sandstone forms narrows and swimming pools of its own. The last mandatory swim is about a mile upstream from trail #17.

To find the route up to trail #17, you'll have to keep track of your progress carefully on the map. Just as the Supai cliff on creek right fades into the hillside, a rudimentary trail leads up and away from the creek, tying in with trail #17 in about 0.5 miles. Trail #17 is a steep 1,700-foot climb to the rim and road #214A.

WEST CLEAR CREEK

lower

General Description: A deep and wild canyon with a trail and a beautiful creek

Best Season: All year, except during high water, most commonly found sometime between early February and early April.

Elevation: 5,800'—3,680' (creek elevation 4,080'—3,680')

Length: 5 miles along creek. Trail #17 climbs about 2 miles from the creek to road #214A.

Time Needed: 3.5—8 hours from the trailhead to Bull Pen Ranch. Or 2 days.

Difficulty: Easy—Moderate. Most of this section has a good trail, but there may be some boulder hopping or wading in the lower portion near Bull Pen, where the trail washes away.

Shuttle: Optional. An easy downhill hike would be from road #214A to Bull Pen, but just going up and back from Bull Pen is nice too.

Maps: USGS: Walker Mtn. 7.5, Buckhorn Mtn. 7.5, USFS: Coconino N.F.

Access: Lower end: From Camp Verde, take highway 260 to the east for about 5 miles to forest road #618. Take road #618 2.2 miles to the Bull Pen Ranch road. Follow this to its end, about another 4 miles.

Upper end: From the junction of road #618 and Bull Pen Ranch road (see above directions), take #618 north for 2 miles to road #214. Make a right on #214 and follow it for 5.3 miles to #214A. Take road #214A about 1.3 miles to the trail #17 parking area. Road #214A is rocky, requiring high clearance vehicles.

Trip Description: This is the mellowest stretch of the West Clear Creek Canyon, but it is still an impressive place. Thick bands of basalt rise imposingly on the rims, and springs form shady green oases on otherwise dry slopes.

In theory, trail #17 leads upstream from Bull Pen Ranch. In reality, floods wash away trail #17 periodically, and the best route is usually up the creekbed. Eventually, the trail is evident only because it traverses the benchland, above the flood plain and out of harm's way. Trail #17 marches through the junipers on the bench on creek right before beginning the steep climb to the rim and road #214A.

The creek along this stretch tumbles through boulders, drifts under sycamore trees, and slides over bedrock slabs of Supai sandstone. The scenery is big in here. Basalt rims rise high above the canyon floor. Numerous springs give life to pockets of alder, cottonwood, sycamore, and oak high on the hillsides. Of course, the cool clear water of the creek is always an attraction.

Tonto Creek Gorge

Swimming "The White Box"

Canyoneering can be an easy stroll down a sandy creekbed.

Warming up on a sun-baked slab

Pumphouse Wash

Ed Price splashes down James Canyon

The trail to Rainbow Bridge

Lisa Gelczis

Canyons offer tranquillity...

...or excitement

Walls streaked in desert varnish are common in Colorado Plateau canyons.

Walking on water

A peaceful scene beneath daunting cliffs of basalt in Wet Beaver Creek

Cross-bedded sandstone near Paria Canyon

A natural waterslide

Lisa Gelczis

Dense forests blanket many Arizona canyons

Parting the slime in the bowels of Salome

Boulder Hopping in West Clear Creek

CHRISTOPHER CREEK

General Description: An accessible canyon with lovely pools and small
waterfalls.
Best Season: May—September
Elevation: 5,760'—4,920'
Length: 1—3 miles
Time Needed: 2 hours—all day
Difficulty: Moderate (wading, scrambling)
Shuttle: No
Maps: USGS: Promontory Butte 7.5, USFS: Tonto N.F.

Access: From the junction of highways 260 and 87 in Payson, head east
on 260 for approximately 19 miles. At 0.1 miles past milepost 271, trail
#298 heads south from the highway. Park here.

Trip Description: Christopher Creek flows through a pine forest below the
Mogollon Rim. Just before the confluence with Tonto Creek, it plunges into
a rugged red-hued gorge. The perennial flow in the creek creates some
beautiful waterfalls and pools as it flows through this gorge. This is a great
place to cool off on a hot day.

From highway 260, walk down trail #298 about a mile to the rim of
the canyon. From here, there are some steep routes on loose rock heading
straight into the canyon. Safer routes are located upstream, where the
creek climbs out of the gorge. In the canyon bottom, you will have to
climb or find routes around several waterfalls if you wish to make your way
downstream. The top few pour-offs and pools are a worthy destination,
however. This canyon isn't long, but with the many clear plungepools and
polished rock, an entire day could easily be spent swimming, lounging,
and climbing through the canyon.

This place occasionally gets trashed on weekends. Please take out any
trash you see, and educate any litterbugs you see.

Christopher Creek Gorge

If you decide to huck your carcass, make sure you hit
deep water or you may become a statistic.

CHRISTOPHER CREEK

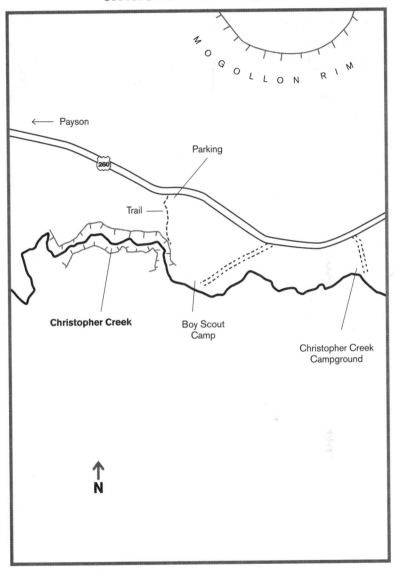

Payson ←

260

Parking

Trail

Christopher Creek

Boy Scout Camp

Christopher Creek Campground

N

main canyon bottom
side canyon bottom
trail
route
paved road
dirt road

tank spring guage

1 mile

TONTO CREEK

General Description: An epic trip through the granddaddy of Mogollon Rim canyons
Best Season: May—September
Elevation: 5,300'—2,950' (creek elevation 3,960'—2,950')
Length: 22 miles
Time Needed: 2.5—4 days
Difficulty: Difficult (swimming, scrambling)
Shuttle: Yes
Maps: USGS: Diamond Butte 7.5, McDonald Mtn. 7.5, Payson So. 7.5, USFS: Tonto N.F.

Access: To get to the lower end where you'll want to leave a vehicle: From the junction of highways 260 and 87 in Payson, take highway 87 south for 11.8 miles and turn east toward Gisela. Follow road 417 past Gisela to a locked gate that marks private property. Park here. This parking area is 6.7 miles from the highway.

For the upper end of the canyon: From the 260 and 87 junction in Payson, take highway 260 east for 11.2 miles to road #405A. The Hellsgate Trailhead is 0.4 miles down #405A on the right.

Trip Description: Tonto Creek is a massive drainage in the heart of the Mogollon Rim country. After heavy rains, it can flow up to 60,000 cubic feet per second—a flow much greater than the Colorado River's average modern-day flow in the Grand Canyon. As you might imagine, a stream with this much potential can cut a rather impressive gorge, and Tonto Creek has done just that. Polished bedrock of granite and rhyolite frames the creek, sometimes constricting it into pools 20 feet deep. The canyon of Tonto Creek is a place where you can feel like you are in another world.

Hellsgate Trail #37 is at first a jeep trail in the pines, then gradually it turns into a foot path and rolls through juniper and pinyon on Apache Ridge. It then switchbacks off the ridge and leads down to the confluence of Tonto and Haigler Creeks. There are several nice campsites here.

As you start downstream along Tonto Creek, don't even try to keep your feet dry, you'll be in the water for most of the next 17 miles. It is best to do this hike when it is hot enough so that getting in the water and swimming is pleasure, not pain. I did this trip during a warm spell in early April. The temperature was in the low 80s, but I would've preferred 90s or even 100 degrees. I spent a lot of time hiking and climbing around trying to avoid swimming. For the record, I ended up having to swim 11 pools. The water temperature usually seems to be in the low 60s.

There are several sections of narrows along Tonto Creek, each with its own character. The pools are nearly nonstop. The geology changes around every other bend. A complex swirl of metamorphic rock underlies the region. My favorite rock group on Tonto Creek is a wonderfully soft, warm, and smooth pink granite that appears briefly toward the lower end of the gorge. There is very little evidence of man in this canyon, not even fire rings. Please try to keep it that way if you decide to visit.

Saguaros begin to appear about 5 miles from the mouth of the canyon. You may sense that you are approaching civilization as the canyon walls begin to recede and you see livestock (or at least signs of it) in an open area known as McDonald Pocket. Surprise! Tonto Creek is not done yet, as you will soon enter "the last hurrah." This final section of canyon begins with a pool stretching over 100 yards long and sitting beneath sheer canyon walls over 200 feet high. After this, the creek begins dropping more steeply and twists and splashes its way through gorgeous white rock before plunging off a 12-foot falls into another deep, green pool. It is a fitting end to the trip to slip into the water at the base of this noisy, spraying falls and let the current push you out into a placid pool at the mouth of the canyon.

You still have a couple of miles of lovely swimming holes before picking up a trail on creek right. Look for a path coming out of the mesquite bosque near the Houston Creek confluence. This will lead you around private property for about 0.5 miles to the road, and trips end.

Try to visit Tonto creek at least 10 days after the last rain. It runs a muddy brown for several days after precipitation, and it is much safer and more pleasant canyoneering to travel through clear water than brown water.

TONTO CREEK

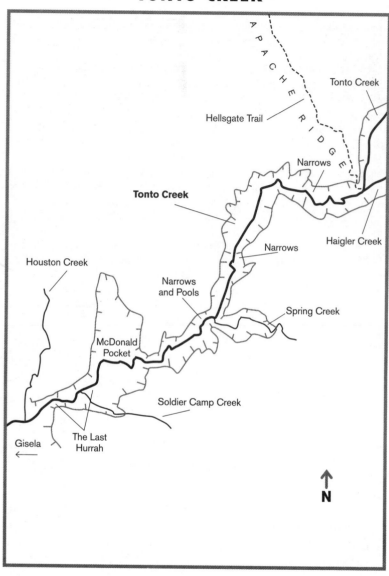

A P A C H E   R I D G E

Tonto Creek

Hellsgate Trail

Narrows

Tonto Creek

Narrows

Haigler Creek

Houston Creek

Narrows

Narrows
and Pools

Spring Creek

McDonald
Pocket

Soldier Camp Creek

Gisela
←

The Last
Hurrah

N

1 mile

main canyon bottom	▬▬▬▬▬
side canyon bottom	─────
trail	- - - - - -
route	··············
paved road	═════
dirt road	·:·:·:·:·:

● tank   ♂ spring   ⊗ guage

Typical Tonto Creek scene

CIBECUE CREEK

General Description: A tributary of the Salt River with spectacular waterfalls
Best Season: April—October
Elevation: 3,100'—2,900'
Length: 6 miles round trip
Time Needed: 1 day
Difficulty: Difficult—Technical (climbing, rappelling)
Shuttle: No
Maps: USGS: Seneca 7.5
USFS: Tonto N.F.
Permits: You must obtain permits for hiking on the Apache Reservation at the Salt River Canyon Store in the Salt River Canyon. As of 1998, **Apache law requires that any canyoneering above the lowest waterfall must be lead by a licensed guide recognized by the White Mountain Apache Tribe. For more information call (520) 338-4385.**

Access: From Globe, take highway 60 north for about 40 miles to the Salt River Canyon. Turn downstream on the river road and follow it 7 miles to Cibecue Creek.

Trip Description: Cibecue Creek plunges toward the Salt River in dramatic fashion in its last few miles. Within the confines of Cibecue you'll find colorful metamorphic rocks and slot canyon narrows, but the real gem of this place is the water. Crystal blue water showers into deep plungepools and cascades over falls up to 50 feet high. When the weather is right, there aren't swimming holes anywhere more inviting than those of Cibecue.

From the parking area near the mouth of Cibecue Creek it is 1 mile of boulder hopping and wading upstream to a pounding waterfall at the rear of this box canyon. These falls are a worthy destination, and serve as a turn around spot for those who are not accompanied by a guide. Guided canyoneers can proceed upstream via a climbing route located just downstream of the falls. Upon your return, you will be faced with a rappel back to the creek.

Once beyond the big falls, there are idyllic pools and several small waterfalls cutting into polished bedrock. The canyon is not narrow here; slopes of juniper replace canyon walls. Accordingly, the technical difficulty is not great, but some scrambling and wading will be necessary to stay near the creek. The pools get more impressive as you go, culminating with a 50-foot waterfall spilling into an unusual set of metamorphic narrows stretching 100 yards. It is not mandatory that you enter the narrows. A route leads around them on creek left, offering a view of the waterfall from above. If you do try to explore the narrows, do so with caution. Only strong canyoneers with some experience around swiftwater should attempt it.

At the flows I have found, the creek is quite powerful in here due to the constriction of the channel. Drowning is a possibility.

There is a picture perfect swimming hole right above the waterfall. Above this, Cibecue loses its gradient and the canyon becomes less spectacular. Return the way you came.

Waterfall on Cibecue Creek

CIBECUE CREEK

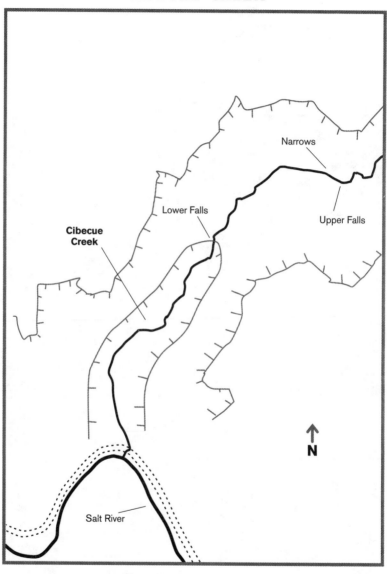

Narrows

Lower Falls

Upper Falls

**Cibecue
Creek**

N

Salt River

1 mile

main canyon bottom	━━━━
side canyon bottom	────
trail	- - - - -
route	··········
paved road	═══
dirt road	- - - - -

tank spring guage

THE RANGES

POLAND CREEK CANYON

General Description: A granite canyon in the rugged southern Bradshaw Mountains

Best Season: March—November (Summer would be hot, but there are swimming possibilities at the bottom.)

Elevation: 5,420'—4,400'

Length: 3 miles round trip

Time Needed: 30 minutes—1.5 hours to the bottom of the canyon; 40 minutes—2.5 hours coming back up

Difficulty: Moderate (rocky trail with 1,000-foot elevation change)

Shuttle: No

Maps: USGS: Crown King 7.5, USFS: Prescott N.F.

Access: Exit I-17 at either the Bumble Bee or Bloody Basin exits. Take road #259 towards Crown King. About 2.5 to 3 miles east of Crown King, there is a wide turnout overlooking the canyon. This is 100 yards downhill of mile marker 25. Park at this turnout.

Trip Description: The eastern flank of the southern Bradshaw Mountains is a rugged, granite studded landscape that serves as the centerpiece for the Castle Creek Wilderness. Poland Creek is the largest drainage in the Castle Creek Wilderness.

Trail #225 drops 1,000 feet through thick chaparral before crossing Poland Creek at 1.5 miles. This spot is one of the several "Hells Holes" in Arizona's canyon country. For down-canyon exploration, start down the creekbed here. The trail heads up Horsethief Canyon and into the Bradshaw Mountains.

The creekbed is mostly granite, with hornblende and schist intrusions. Pools of water are plentiful except in the driest of times. I was here after 2 months of nearly no rain, and there were still several pools big enough for a refreshing dip. Downstream from Hells Hole on Poland Creek, there is a fall with a pool at the bottom, forming one of the nicest swimming holes anywhere.

This region receives more thunderstorm activity than most of central Arizona, so be aware of the weather when you're here, especially during the summer monsoon season.

POLAND CREEK

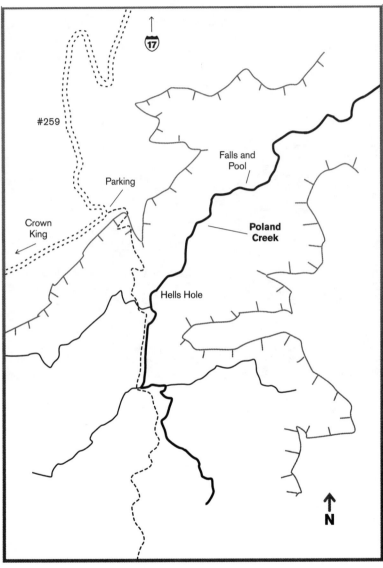

#259

Crown
King

Parking

Falls and
Pool

**Poland
Creek**

Hells Hole

N

main canyon bottom
side canyon bottom
trail
route
paved road
dirt road

tank spring guage

1 mile

Ken Webb surveys the swimming hole in Poland Creek Canyon.

AGUA FRIA RIVER CANYON

General Description: A saguaro filled canyon with a running stream
Best Season: March, April, May, October, November
Elevation: 3,100'—2,500'
Length: 10.5 miles round trip from Badger Springs Wash to Sunset Pt. Canyon
Time Needed: 4.5—10 hours for the round trip
Difficulty: Moderate (scrambling, wading)
Shuttle: Optional
Maps: USGS: Joes Hill 7.5, USFS: Prescott N.F.

Access: Take the Badger Springs Exit 256 off I-17. Drive to the southeast towards the canyon, which you can see about a mile away. There are many dirt roads here, but they all head towards Badger Springs Wash. Four wheel drives can make it all the way to the wash, two wheel drives will have to park about 0.3 miles short of the wash.

If you want to run a shuttle, you can park a vehicle just east of the freeway at the Sunset Point Exit.

Trip Description: The Agua Fria is a gem of a desert canyon. It is hard to believe that the interstate is only one air mile away when you are standing in the sandy river bottom of this quiet canyon.

From your parking spot near Badger Springs exit, walk down Badger Springs Wash to the Agua Fria River. The bottom of this canyon is granite, sitting below rocky saguaro-studded slopes beneath a basalt rim. The river may dry up in severe droughts, but there is usually water in this canyon section. Proceeding downstream, you will be scrambling around, over, and under polished gray and white boulders that surround lovely pools. The water temperature is relatively warm, making wading and splashing in the creek delightful. In places you'll want to walk across the huge beaches of sand and driftwood, evidence of the floods that sometimes rage through this canyon. About 2.5 miles down from Badger Springs Wash, the canyon begins to narrow, and only some creative scrambling will keep your feet out of the water. Just below Perry Tank Creek, where the river makes a 90-degree turn to the right, there is a pool that is a mandatory wade, as the canyon walls rise straight out of the riverbed. Below this it is again a babbling brook amongst large boulders until an unnamed side canyon enters from the west, which we'll call Sunset Point Canyon, because its origin is at the Sunset Point Overlook.

Below Sunset Point Canyon, the Agua Fria Canyon widens and much of the water goes under the sand. This is a good turnaround spot. Or, if you've set up a shuttle, hike up Sunset Point Canyon to your vehicle.

AGUA FRIA

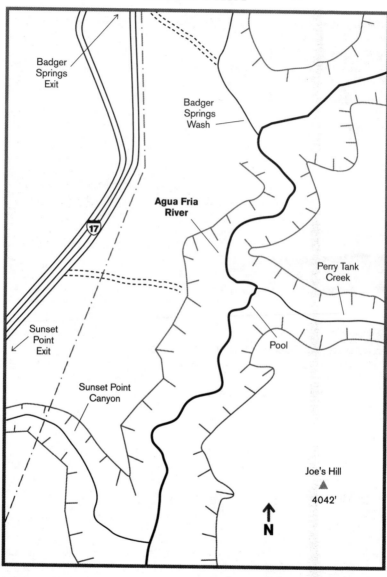

Badger
Springs
Exit

Badger
Springs
Wash

**Agua Fria
River**

17

Perry Tank
Creek

Sunset
Point
Exit

Pool

Sunset Point
Canyon

Joe's Hill

4042'

N

1 mile

main canyon bottom	————
side canyon bottom	———
trail	- - - - - - - -
route	··················
paved road	════════
dirt road	┄┄┄┄┄┄┄

●   ♂   ⊗
tank   spring   guage

Clear water and saguaro cactus—an incongruous scene.

BILL WILLIAMS RIVER CANYON

General Description: A permanent stream in a desert canyon
Best Season: October—March
Elevation: 1,278'—900'
Time Needed: 5.5—9 hours, or 2 days
Length: 11 miles round trip
Difficulty: Moderate (wading, swimming or climbing)
Shuttle: No
Maps: USGS: Alamo Dam 7.5, Reid Valley 7.5

Access: From Wenden, head north on Alamo Lake Road to Alamo Lake State Park. Drive west towards the dam. There is fee parking at the Bill Williams Overlook.

Trip Description: From the overlook, walk down the road that leads to the gaging station below the dam. There is an intimidating gate blocking this road, but hikers may pass. In the canyon bottom a pleasant stream runs through the Sonoran Desert between slopes of colorful metamorphic rock. There is a variety of birdlife as well, although much of the riparian habitat was wiped out in the floods of 1993. There is one pool not far below the gauge where you might have to swim. If you're not prepared for swimming, there is a climbing route (5.1) around this pool on the right. Below here it is flat easy walking, though you must cross the stream several times.

About 5 miles down from the dam, the Bill Williams River leaves its canyon and enters a wide valley. You could hike this entire canyon and return to your car in a day, but with the many campsites and isolation you'll find, two days is nicer.

If the weather has been wet recently, check the USGS water resources page on the internet and find out how much water they are releasing from the dam. The standard release is 25 cubic feet per second. Hiking here could be dangerous if the flow is over 50 c.f.s.

The lower end of Bill Williams River Canyon

BILL WILLIAMS

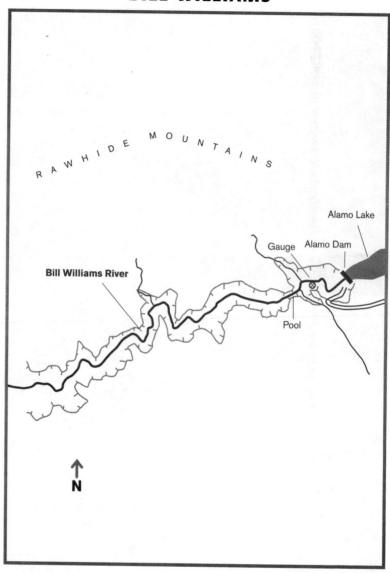

R A W H I D E   M O U N T A I N S

Alamo Lake

Gauge   Alamo Dam

Bill Williams River

Pool

N

1 mile

main canyon bottom	————————
side canyon bottom	————————
trail	- - - - - - - - - -
route	··························
paved road	═══════════
dirt road	┄┄┄┄┄┄┄

tank   spring   guage

A side canyon along the Bill Williams River

PALM CANYON

General Description: A short hike to the only native palm trees in Arizona
Elevation: 2,400'—2,100'
Best Season: November—March
Length: 0.8 miles one way to view the palms
Time Needed: 30 minutes—2 hours
Difficulty: Easy
Shuttle: No
Maps: USGS: Palm Canyon 7.5

Access: Exit I-10 at Quartzite and drive south on highway 95 for approximately 20 miles. Turn east onto a dirt road toward the Kofa Mountains and Palm Canyon and follow it to its end.

Trip Description: The Kofa Mountains provide a dramatic craggy skyline in the heart of the Sonoran Desert. Within these desert mountains is a steep little drainage that is home to two dozen or so palm trees. It is an unexpected sight in one of the driest and hottest places in North America.

From the parking area, a trail leads up the canyon to a spot for viewing the largest grove of palms. The palms are *Washingtonia filifera*, or California Washingtonias, named for our first president. This species of palm is commonly seen in Arizona, but the only place they grow naturally in our state is here in the Kofa Mountains.

If you get an early start, you may see desert bighorn sheep cruising the rocky slopes. Palm Canyon lies within the Kofa National Wildlife Refuge.

Palm trees in the desert

PALM CANYON

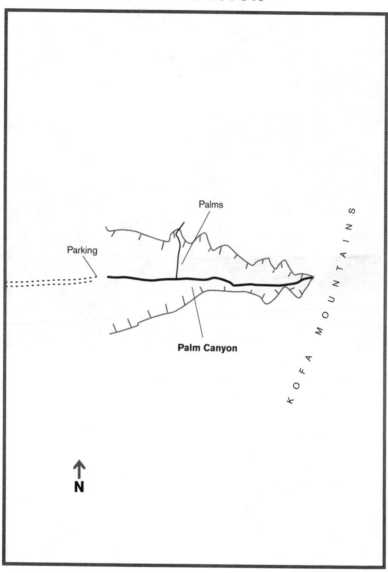

Palms

Parking

Palm Canyon

K O F A   M O U N T A I N S

N

1 mile

main canyon bottom	
side canyon bottom	
trail	- - - - - - - - - - - -
route	....
paved road	
dirt road	

tank   spring   guage

Lisa Gelczis

Desert Bighorn

SALOME CREEK

General Description: A designated wilderness canyon with spectacular pools and isolation

Best Season: March—May, October, November. I did this trip in March. There was plenty of water all the way, but air and water temperatures were too cold for swimming. Climbing around pools was a hassle and exploring "The Jug" was not an option. May might be a good month, but the creek could be mostly dry by June. Optimum would be a steady flow in the creek with air temperatures in the 90s. These conditions probably rarely exist.

Elevation: 6,000'—2,500'

Length: 22 miles

Time Needed: 3 or 4 days

Difficulty: Difficult (wading, possible swimming, route finding)

Shuttle: Yes

Maps: USGS: Copper Mtn. 7.5, Armer Mtn. 7.5, USFS: Tonto N.F.

Access: Upper End: Take the Young Highway (route 288) to Reynolds Creek Campground. Start hiking down trail #284.

Lower End: Take AZ Highway 188 about 8 miles south of Punkin Center. At milepost 255, take road #60 (also known as A Cross Road) to the east for 10.1 miles. Park at "The Jug" trailhead.

Trip Description: Salome Creek drains a good portion of the Sierra Ancha mountains. It plunges through granite gorges, spreads out amongst broad mesquite bosques, and provides a pleasant babbling brook in the desert before emptying into Roosevelt Reservoir.

To begin your descent into upper Salome, take trail #284 from Reynolds Creek Campground. This trail winds through a ponderosa pine forest and passes the Armer Ranch before finally making a steep descent through chaparral to a place called "Hells Hole" on Workman Creek. There is a wonderful campsite at the bottom.

A trail goes along a bench about 200 feet above the south side of Workman Creek. This trail heads toward Salome Creek, but it quickly degenerates into a game trail. You may have to do some bushwhacking to get into the creekbed of Salome. Once in the creekbed of Salome, you might have to wade or swim in places, depending on water level. The same type of granite that forms "The Jug," which lies downstream, appears here, creating scenic pools.

A few miles below the Salome-Workman creeks confluence, the canyon begins to open. From here downstream to "The Jug," your route is either in the creekbed, or in thickets of mesquite that line the stream. These riparian zones harbor a variety of birdlife. I saw an eagle at close range in one of these thickets—an impressive sight.

As Dutchwoman Butte begins to rise to the east of the creek, Salome begins its plunge into "The Jug." This is a spectacular granite gorge that requires a favorable water level and at least one rappel to descend. For more details, consult the Salome Jug description.

At "The Jug," you can pick up a jeep trail on creek right that leads about 1.7 miles to A Cross Road, and your shuttle vehicle.

Ken Webb

Polished granite and clear pools dot the course of Salome Creek.

SALOME CREEK

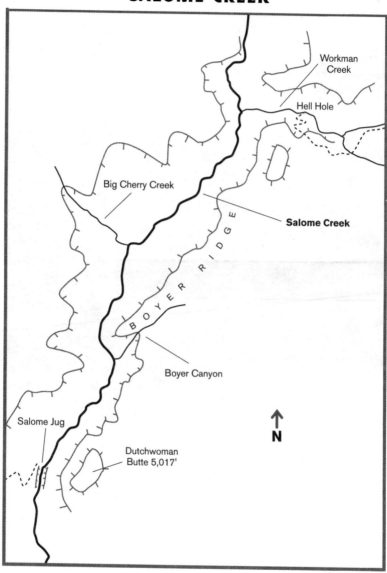

Workman
Creek

Hell Hole

Big Cherry Creek

Salome Creek

B O Y E R   R I D G E

Boyer Canyon

N

Salome Jug

Dutchwoman
Butte 5,017'

1 mile

main canyon bottom	———————
side canyon bottom	———————
trail	- - - - - - - - -
route	··················
paved road	════════
dirt road	┄┄┄┄┄┄┄

tank   spring   guage

Salome Creek Wilderness

SALOME JUG

"The Jug"

General Description: A spectacular granite gorge
Best Season: May, June, mid-September—October
Elevation: 2,700'—2,500'
Length: 5 miles round trip
Time Needed: 1 day
Difficulty: Technical
Shuttle: No
Maps: USGS: Armer Mtn. 7.5, USFS: Tonto N.F.

Access: Take highway 188 south from Punkin Center about 8 miles. Near milepost 255, take road #60 (also known as A Cross Road) to the east for 10.1 miles. Park at "The Jug" trailhead.

Trip Description: When I originally set out to write this book, I wasn't going to include this canyon. I thought that such an incredible place with such easy access ran a great risk of overuse and exploitation. I thought it was best left a secret. But now, 7 years after my first visit to "The Jug", and before this book has gone to print, it seems the secret is out. I have seen information about "The Jug" published more than once in national magazines, and I've even noticed hiking clubs in Phoenix advertising trips to "The Jug." So as long as this place is no longer a private stash, I may as well try to promote safe, responsible, and respectful use of the place.

Since "The Jug" is only two easy miles from a road, it attracts a wide range of people. Always pick up any trash you see, both on the hike in, or certainly in "The Jug" itself. If you see anyone in this cathedral who is not treating it with the respect it deserves, please educate them.

Water levels change the character of "The Jug" dramatically. Low water levels dry up the flow of water in the creek, isolating the pools. This turns a clear, clean pool into stagnant water that collects a particulate film, usually in some shade of green. Sounds appealing, eh? Well, at least by gritting your teeth and breast stroking through the scum, you can still explore the place. At high water, you can't even do that. The boulder scrambles of low water turn into deadly torrents of bone-chilling whitewater. How much water is too much? Only someone with an experienced eye for whitewater can make an accurate judgement. If you are unsure, it is probably too high. A very small amount of water, if constricted and hurtled downhill, can be deadly.

Like most Arizona rivers and streams, the water levels here are erratic. Perfect, medium water levels are hard to find. Good luck in catching a perfectly moderate water level. I've been here 4 times, and only caught it once. In the following description, the creek is at that elusive perfect water level.

It is a 2 mile walk down an abandoned dirt road to the head of "The Jug." You will be able to see the gorge as you approach. This gorge would be an amazing place regardless of its rock type. "The Jug," however, is extra special due to the pink-hued polished granite forming the marble smooth canyon walls. Near the top of the gorge, cattails grow along placid pools encased in granite. As Salome Creek begins to plummet into the bowels of the earth, slippery slides offer the only access downstream. At the bottom of the slides, rippling clear pools stretch from wall to vertical wall. Wading and swimming are essentially the only means of travel through most of the gorge. Occasionally, a sun-warmed slab of granite will present itself as a hot plate, perfect for reheating your wet body.

Towards the lower end of the gorge, there is a 20-foot waterfall. At the right water level, you can take an adrenaline filled leap into the pool at the base of these falls. If the water is low, a bolt placed to the right of the falls provides an anchor for rappelling.

A long pool sits at the bottom of the waterfall, one of the last swims in "The Jug." Not far below here the smooth canyon walls halt, and the Sonoran Desert surrounds Salome Creek. A steep hike up the creek right slope will bring you back to the abandoned dirt road that leads back to A Cross Road.

Lisa Gelczis

Rappelling in "The Jug"

SALOME JUG

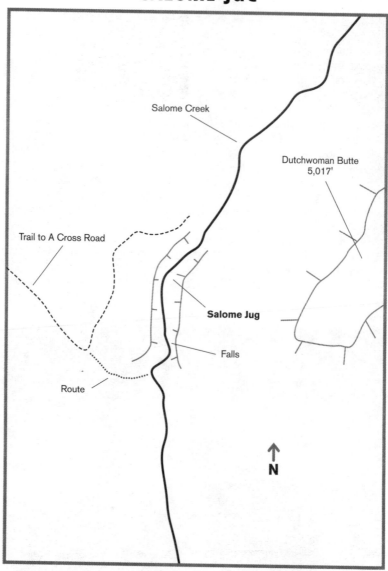

Salome Creek

Dutchwoman Butte
5,017'

Trail to A Cross Road

Salome Jug

Falls

Route

↑
N

1 mile

main canyon bottom	▬▬▬▬
side canyon bottom	─────
trail	- - - - - - -
route	··················
paved road	═════
dirt road	▪▪▪▪▪▪

●   ⚲   ⊗
tank   spring   guage

Swimming in "The Jug"

FISH CREEK CANYON

lower

General Description: A rugged desert canyon in the Superstition
 Mountains
Best Season: October—April
Elevation: 2,100'—1,700'
Length: 8 miles round trip
Time Needed: 4—8 hours
Difficulty: Moderate (boulder hopping)
Shuttle: Optional
Maps: USGS: Horse Mesa Dam 7.5, USFS: Tonto N.F.

Access: From Apache Junction, take the Apache Trail, highway 88, northeast for about 25 miles to where the road crosses Fish Creek. From the
bridge over Fish Creek, continue another 0.7 miles to a parking area on
the north side of the road.

Trip Description: This description is for the section of Fish Creek Canyon
that is downstream of the Apache Trail Road. This canyon leads through
massively rugged country in its descent to the Salt River.
   For about the first mile, the canyon might be waterless. Have faith;
unless you are in the midst of a drought, water will begin to surface as you
travel downstream. There are usually a couple of pools deep enough for a
refreshing dip. The canyon meanders beneath huge mesas guarded by
faces of sheer rock, and it gets narrow for a brief section, but the main
attraction is the big rugged desert towering above.
   When you see powerlines and a road coming into the canyon, it is time
to turn around. The road parallels the creek for the last mile to the Salt
River. If you wanted to do a shuttle, you could leave a vehicle on this road.

Kaibab the wonder dog explores Fish Creek.

FISH CREEK (lower)

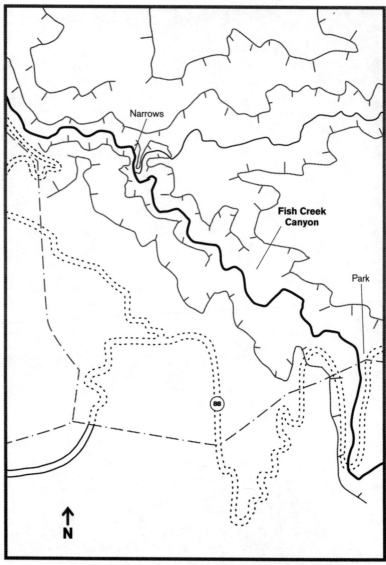

Narrows

Fish Creek
Canyon

Park

88

N

1 mile

main canyon bottom	———
side canyon bottom	——
trail	- - - - - - -
route	··············
paved road	═══════
dirt road	:::::::::

tank spring guage

Fish Creek Canyon gouges the rugged Superstition Mountains.

FISH CREEK CANYON

upper

General Description: A boulder strewn canyon with pools and greenery in the majestic Superstition Wilderness
Best Season: All year
Elevation: 2,800'—2,100'
Length: 6 miles round trip
Time Needed: 4—7 hours
Difficulty: Moderate (scrambling, climbing)
Shuttle: No
Maps: USGS: Horse Mesa Dam 7.5, USFS: Tonto N.F.

Access: From Apache Junction, take highway 88—the Apache Trail—for about 25 miles to the bridge over Fish Creek. Park here.

Trip Description: Stately saguaros standing before a backdrop of huge canyon walls—this is the image that comes to mind when I think of Fish Creek Canyon. Any canyoneer driving along the Apache Trail would be intrigued by the narrow canyon of Fish Creek as it runs beneath the road.

Fish Creek Canyon is a rugged place. Even so, on weekends in the spring, when the pools are flush with water, this canyon can attract a crowd. House-sized boulders fill the creekbed, requiring some scrambling and even some fifth class climbing to proceed upstream. Progress is slow due to all the route exploring and climbing necessary to make it through the boulder jams. The difficulty of travel, of course, is a bonus to those who do make it far, because human traffic is less.

There are numerous pools in the canyon, depending on the season. Early spring after a wet winter would probably be an optimal time to visit, as there may even be a running stream then. Usually there is not so much water in the canyon that you must get wet, but there is enough for a cool dunk when the weather is hot, making this one of the few canyons that can be explored in any season. Surrounding the pools are cottonwoods, sycamores, cattails, and enough other green stuff to keep a botanist busy.

The turnaround point is arbitrary. I headed back downstream after about 3 miles. Trails leading to various locales in the Superstitions enter the canyon about 4 miles up from the road.

FISH CREEK (upper)

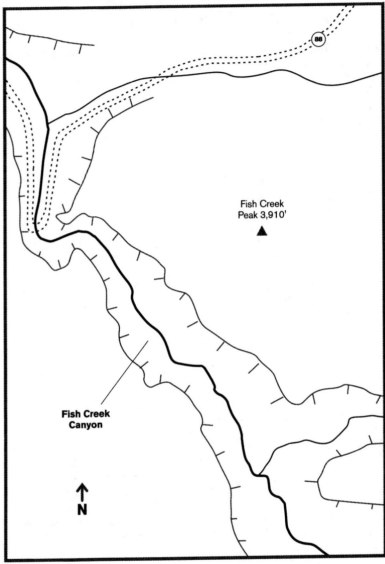

88

Fish Creek
Peak 3,910'
▲

**Fish Creek
Canyon**

↑
N

main canyon bottom	————————
side canyon bottom	————————
trail	- - - - - - - - -
route	·················
paved road	═══════════
dirt road	= = = = = = = =

1 mile

●   ♂   ⊗
tank   spring   guage

DEVILS CANYON

General Description: A canyon in the Pinal mountains with dense riparian zones, falls, and pools
Best Season: mid-May to September (85 degrees or hotter)
Elevation: 4,000'—3,100'
Length: 7 miles round trip
Time Needed: 5—10 hours to the five pools and back
Difficulty: Difficult—Technical
Shuttle: No
Maps: USGS: Superior 7.5, (Teapot Mtn. 7.5), USFS: Tonto N.F.

Access: There are several ways to get into Devils Canyon. You could park near the highway 60 bridge and start downstream, or you could use a trail into the canyon near Oak Flat Campground. The route described here will get you into the neatest part of the canyon via a rough road and a beautiful side canyon.

From Superior, take highway 60 about 4 miles east to Magma Mine Road and a sign for Oak Flat Campground at milepost 231. Turn south on Magma Mine Road, and continue on this paved road for 1.6 miles. At 1.6 miles from the highway, there is a dirt road on the left with a barbed wire gate across it. Take this rocky road for 1.7 miles and park near a cow tank in the Rancho Rio creek bottom.

En route to this parking spot you will pass a pond shortly after leaving the pavement. The road is barely drivable for two wheel drives. Good clearance is a must. Four wheel drives are recommended. Just past the parking spot in Rancho Rio, the road gets extremely rough, absolute 4-wheel-drive territory.

Trip Description: Devils Canyon—it may seem devilish to the unprepared, but to an experienced canyoneer the place seems more heavenly than devilish. Interesting rock formations called "hoodoos" stand guard over this desert drainage full of greenery and deep pools.

From the parking spot at Rancho Rio Tank, the quickest approach to the canyon is down Rancho Rio Creek. Simply walk downstream from the parking spot in the Rancho Rio creek bottom. This route can be cluttered with chaparral, but by staying in the main creek channel, you should be able to keep the bushwhacking to a minimum. There are usually some small pools in Rancho Rio Creek. One of these pools might require a wade. As you near the confluence with Devils Canyon, neat rock formations surround, but there are no obstructions.

Devils Canyon is usually dry for the first 100 yards below Rancho Rio Creek, then water surfaces, supporting a riparian forest. Arizona alders, sycamores, and cottonwood trees form a dense canopy which lends itself to probably the healthiest stands of poison ivy in Arizona. Maybe the blue ribbon poison ivy thickets have something to do with the name of this canyon. If you don't know what poison ivy looks like, don't touch anything green.

Occasionally, the forest stops and rocky cliffs dramatically change the scene. Pools framed by polished bedrock may require a swim or at least a wade. These sections of rock-framed creek don't last long, however. The rocky cliffs quickly relent to the jungle of alder.

When the canyon makes an abrupt turn to the east and begins to plummet, you'll know you've reached the "Five Pools." The Five Pools is a section of canyon which drops 240 feet in 0.2 miles. There are 5 big, deep plunge pools here, below trickling (or sometimes dry) falls. Unless you are comfortable scrambling with exposure, and climbing short pitches of 5.0, your canyon exploration ends here.

You will need 200 feet of rope to make a controlled descent of all 5 falls. Be prepared to make your own anchors for these rappels. The drops range from 12 to 60 feet in height, and the pools range from 40 to 120 feet in diameter. The third fall and pool are the biggest.

The first fall has a fixed rope in it to aid with the downclimb. This rope could wash away with the next flash flood, so bring your own. Once below the roped downclimb, a short scramble will have you at the lip of the second fall. To descend this, rappel the 12 feet or jump into the plunge pool. If you're not prepared to rappel all 5 falls, there is a scrambler's route below this second pool, on the left. This route descends a slope of rock on creek left all the way to the bottom of the five pools. This route can also serve as a return route if you have rappelled into all 5 pools. Remember that this is an out and back trip, so don't go down anything you can't get back up.

On the way back to your vehicle, you may want to explore one of the several side canyons that enter Devils.

DEVILS CANYON

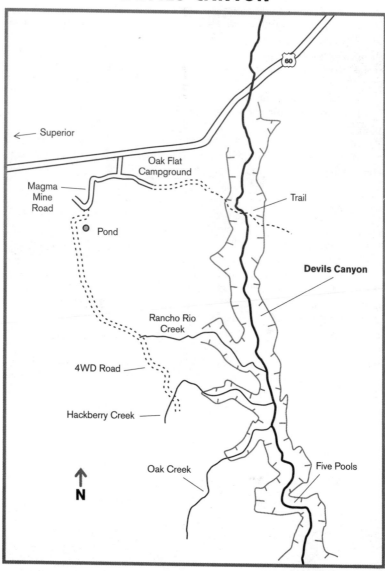

Superior ←

Oak Flat
Campground

Magma
Mine
Road

Pond

Trail

Devils Canyon

Rancho Rio
Creek

4WD Road

Hackberry Creek

Oak Creek

Five Pools

N

1 mile

main canyon bottom	————————
side canyon bottom	————————
trail	- - - - - - - - -
route	··················
paved road	————————
dirt road	∷∷∷∷∷∷∷

tank   spring   guage

A small waterfall in Devils Canyon

ARAVAIPA CANYON

General Description: A permanent clear stream supporting a lush riparian habitat in the Sonoran Desert
Best Season: April, May, September, October
Elevation: 3,000'—2,600'
Length: 10.5 miles end to end
Time Needed: 2 or 3 days. You could do it in 1 long day if you went one way.
Difficulty: Easy
Shuttle: Optional
Maps: USGS: Booger Canyon 7.5, Brandenburg Mtn. 7.5, USFS: Coronado N.F.
Permit: B.L.M. - Safford office (520) 348-4400

Access: For the more easily accessible west entrance, take AZ highway 177 south out of Superior, 32 miles to Winkleman. Continue south on highway 77 for 10.8 miles to Aravaipa Canyon Road. Follow Aravaipa Canyon Road 12 miles to the B.L.M. trailhead.

For the east entrance, take Klondyke Road off highway 70 about 13 miles northeast of Safford. Follow this dirt road to Klondyke and then on to the canyon. The B.L.M. sends directions with your permit.

Trip Description: Aravaipa Canyon is one of Arizona's most popular places to backpack, and once you've been there, it's easy to see why. The desert stream with a sandy bottom is the centerpiece of the canyon, supporting a healthy environment for birds and other wildlife. It flows at a swift pace all year long, and can flash flood at times, as is evidenced by the debris left 20 feet above the normal creek level in places.

Perhaps the most impressive thing about Aravaipa is the lush greenery. Huge cottonwood trees shade picture perfect campsites, and mesquite and sycamore trees form bright green surroundings in the spring. Birders will be kept busy here, there are dozens of species in the area from canyon wrens to Mexican blackhawks.

This is a relatively easy canyon to explore, you'll be walking along a flat, sandy steambed most of the time.

There are several side canyons worth exploring, so give yourself 3 days in Aravaipa if you can.

The B.L.M. limits the number of visitors to Aravaipa Canyon. You must get a permit through the B.L.M. in Safford. Call months ahead of time; permits go fast.

Aravaipa Canyon

Splashing down Aravaipa Creek

Lisa Gelczis

ARAVAIPA

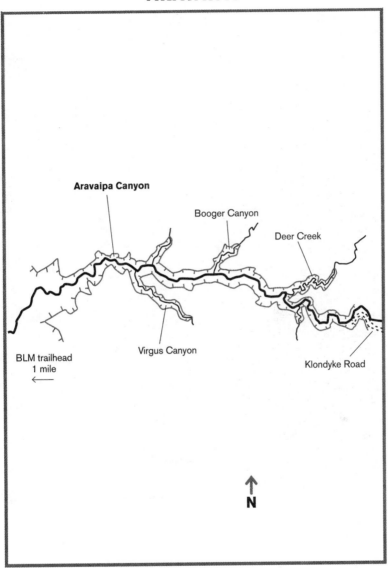

Aravaipa Canyon

Booger Canyon

Deer Creek

BLM trailhead
1 mile
←

Virgus Canyon

Klondyke Road

N

main canyon bottom
side canyon bottom
trail
route
paved road
dirt road

tank spring guage

1 mile

HOT SPRINGS CANYON

General Description: A nice little stream plunging through the Sonoran desert
Best Season: October, November, March—June. Winters might be a bit chilly, but could be nice. Summers have flash flood danger.
Elevation: 4,000'—3,400'
Length: 12 miles round trip
Time Needed: Through the canyon and back would be a full day for a strong hiker: 7—12 hours. Two days is just right for most of us.
Difficulty: Moderate (wading, scrambling)
Shuttle: No
Maps: USGS: Soza Mesa 7.5, Winchester Mtns. 1:62,500, USFS: Coronado N.F. (Safford and Santa Catalina Ranger Districts)

Access: Take the airport road west out of Willcox. This is Cascabel Road. Head west on Cascabel Road about 14 miles to Muleshoe Ranch Road. Head northwest another 14 miles to Muleshoe Ranch Preserve. There are several ranch roads in the vicinity. When in doubt, stay on the main road. The last 14 miles into Muleshoe Ranch gets really muddy after a rain. Try to make your trip on dry roads.

Trip Description: Hot Springs Canyon is another one of those quaint and beautiful little canyons that hides in the rolling hill country of southern Arizona. There are plenty of pleasant 65 degree pools between smooth bedrock walls, but you never have to get more than your ankles wet. Tread lightly, you'll be sharing the pools with the endangered longfin dace. Much of the riparian habitat in the area is owned by The Nature Conservancy. Check in at the Muleshoe Ranch Preserve before setting out. Dogs are not allowed.

From Muleshoe Ranch Preserve, walk downstream to reach Hot Springs Canyon. The footing is river cobbles. For about the first 2 miles downstream from Muleshoe, you are on Nature Conservancy land. As you make your way through dense riparian groves of cottonwoods and mesquite, it's easy to understand why the Conservancy obtained this biologically diverse property. Water is intermittent in the creekbed until about 1.3 miles down from Muleshoe, when a side creek on the right enters with a permanent flow.

About 2 miles down, the canyon really begins as the jungle of riparian vegetation relents to a rocky gorge. Where vegetation is present, it is juniper on the north-facing slopes, and saguaros on the southern exposures. Campsites are small, but scenic. Mini beaches tuck beneath the dark bedrock that envelopes Hot Springs Creek.

Continuing downstream, the canyon walls begin to fade back into the desert. Huge shade-giving cottonwoods line the sandy creekbottom. At the canyon's mouth, a barbed wire fence crosses the stream. This is the turnaround point.

Don't come to Hot Springs Creek expecting to find hot springs. The only geothermal activity near here is back at Muleshoe, where you can enjoy the natural hot water only if you stay in a rented casita at the preserve.

Lisa Gelczis

Hot Springs Creek is not hot water.

HOT SPRINGS

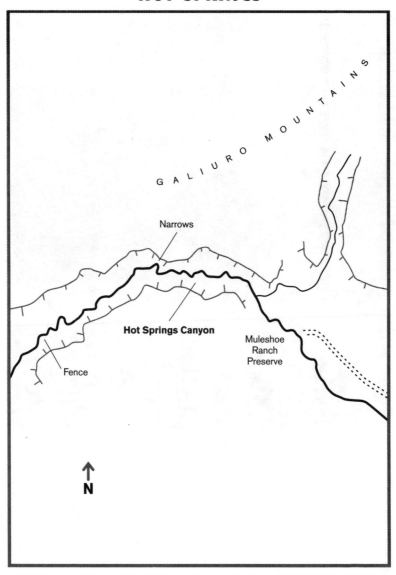

GALIURO MOUNTAINS

Narrows

Hot Springs Canyon

Muleshoe
Ranch
Preserve

Fence

N

1 mile

main canyon bottom	▬▬▬
side canyon bottom	▬▬▬
trail	- - - - - -
route	··············
paved road	══════
dirt road	-------

tank   spring   guage

Lisa Gelczis

Driftwood serves as a flash flood testimonial.

SYCAMORE CREEK

General Description: A pleasant canyon near the Mexican border with a perennial stream

Best Season: Mid-September through June. Sunny winter days are lovely here. With the available water, the heat of early summer would be tolerable. The middle of summer is probably okay, too, but the plentiful thunderstorms of this season pose a flash flood threat.

Elevation: 4,000'—3,480'

Length: 9 miles round trip to the international border

Time Needed: 4—9 hours

Difficulty: Moderate (scrambling, possible wading)

Shuttle: No

Maps: USGS: Ruby 7.5, USFS: Coronado N.F. (south)

Access: From Tucson, take I-19 south about 55 miles to the route 289 junction at exit 12. Head west on route 289. About 10 miles from the freeway, bear left, towards Arivaca. The road to the right goes to Pena Blanca Lake. Proceed down the dirt road toward Arivaca for 9 miles, where you will cross Sycamore Creek. Turn left, following the creekbed downstream for 0.3 miles to a parking area.

Trip Description: Sycamore Canyon is home to a lovely perennial stream between steep hillsides of ocotillo, oak, juniper, and chaparral. Dramatic rocky outcrops keep the scenery interesting. There is one short stretch of narrows and enough deep pools for a refreshing dip.

Immediately downstream from the parking area, a trail snakes its way between meanders in the creekbed. This trail is evident throughout the gentler parts of this canyon. When things get more rugged, the trail disappears.

The first challenge to downstream travel is also home to one of the loveliest pools in the canyon. A wall of rhyolite intersects the canyon bottom, allowing only the incessant flow of water to pass through a gap in the wall. To negotiate this impediment, either follow the water and swim a pool, or take the scrambler's route to the right. A few carefully placed rocks may help you maintain dry feet in bypassing this pool.

Not far below this, a brief narrow section of canyon emerges. Note the flash flood testimonial in here: a mature cottonwood tree spanning the canyon, wedged solidly between the walls 15 feet above the creek. In this narrow spot you will have a deep wade or swim, unless you make the scramble to the right of the pool.

Below the narrows, the creek continues to meander along, creating some nice pools en route to the Mexican border a few miles distant. Campsites are not hard to find. Some side canyons come in, occasionally adding flow to Sycamore Creek.

This is an out and back journey, so your turnaround point is arbitrary. If you reach a fence crossing the creek and indicating the international border, I would recommend a turnaround.

The narrows of Sycamore Creek

SYCAMORE CREEK

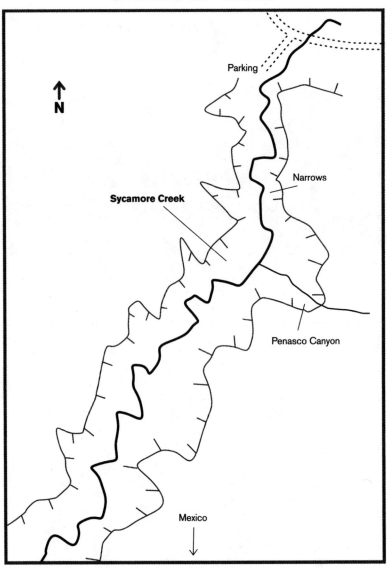

Parking

Narrows

Sycamore Creek

Penasco Canyon

Mexico

N

1 mile

main canyon bottom	
side canyon bottom	
trail	
route	
paved road	
dirt road	

tank   spring   guage

APPENDIX

GLOSSARY OF CANYONEERING TERMS

Alluvium: Any stream-laid sediment, found in a stream channel.

Colluvium: Deposit of sediment or rock particles accumulated at the base of a slope.

Confluence: A flowing together of two or more streambeds.

Fall(s): A drop-off in the riverbed. A fall is the same as a waterfall, except a fall is usually dry, whereas a waterfall has water.

Narrows: A section of canyon where the canyon walls are significantly close together. This is a subjective term. Generally, this term is applied to any piece of canyon that conveys a sense of confinement.

Riparian zone: The area near the bank of a river or streambed. Riparian vegetation is that which grows only where it can gain water from the stream.

Route: A way from one place to another. In canyoneering, a route is often a way through the cliffs that form the canyon.

Side drainage: A creekbed, gully, ditch, or some type of watercourse that is a tributary of the more major riverbed.

HELPFUL PHONE NUMBERS

Apache-Sitgreaves National Forest
309 South Mountain Avenue
P.O. Box 640
Springerville, AZ 85938
(520) 333-4301

Alpine Ranger District (520) 339-4384
Clifton Ranger District (520) 687-1301
Chevelon-Heber Ranger Districts (520) 535-4481
Springerville Ranger District (520) 333-4372
Lakeside Ranger District (520) 368-5111

Coconino National Forest
2323 E. Greenlaw Lane
Flagstaff, AZ 86004
(520) 527-3600

Beaver Creek Ranger District (520) 567-4121
Peaks Ranger District (520) 526-0866
Happy Jack Information Center (520) 477-2172
Mormon Lake Ranger District (520) 774-1147
Sedona Ranger District (520) 282-4119
Mogollon Rim Center (520) 477-2255

Coronado National Forest
Federal Building, 300 W. Congress
Tuscon, AZ 85701
(520) 670-4552

Douglas Ranger District (520) 364-3468
Nogales Ranger District (520) 281-2296
Sierra Vista Ranger District (520) 378-0311
Safford Ranger District (520) 428-4150
Santa Catalina Ranger District (520) 749-8700

Kaibab National Forest
800 South 6th Street
Williams, AZ 86046
(520) 635-8200

Williams Ranger District (520) 635-2633
Chalender Ranger District (520) 635-2676
North Kaibab Ranger District (520) 643-7395
Tusayan Ranger District (520) 638-2443

Prescott National Forest
344 South Cortez Street
Prescott, AZ 86303-4398
(520) 771-4700

Chino Valley Ranger District (520) 636-2302
Verde Ranger District (520) 567-4121

Tonto National Forest
2324 E. McDowell Road
Phoenix, AZ 85006
(602) 225-5200

Cave Creek Ranger District (602) 488-3441
Globe Ranger District (520) 402-6200
Mesa Ranger District (602) 379-6446
Payson Ranger District (520) 474-7900
Pleasant Valley Ranger District (520) 462-4300
Tonto Basin Ranger District (520) 467-3200

Bureau of Land Management
Arizona B.L.M. office
222 N. Central Avenue
Phoenix, AZ 85004-3208
P.O. Box 555
Phoenix, AZ 85001-0555
(602) 417-9504

Safford B.L.M
711 14th Avenue
Safford, AZ 85546
(520) 348-4400

Navajo Nation
Cameron Visitor Center
P.O. Box 549
Cameron, AZ 86020
(520) 679-2303

Lechee Sub-Office (520) 698-3360
*Water Holes Canyon information
*Antelope Canyon information

Parks and Recreation Department
P.O. Box 9000
Window Rock, AZ 86515
(520) 871-6647

Ranger Headquarters (520) 871-6701

White Mountain Apache Tribe
Game and Fish Department
(520) 338-4385
*Cibecue Creek information

Hon-Dah Recreation (520) 369-7669

Hualapai Tribe
(520) 769-2219

State Land Departments
Phoenix (602) 542-2119
Tucson (520) 628-6015
Flagstaff (520) 774-1425
Prescott (520) 778-9567
Pinetop (520) 367-0313

FLAGSTAFF AREA SHOPS & SERVICES

PHOENIX AREA SHOPS & SERVICES